HILLTOP
DRIVE

JOE JACHENS

ISBN 978-1-0980-3369-9 (paperback)
ISBN 978-1-0980-3370-5 (digital)

Christian Faith Publishing, Inc.
832 Park Avenue
Meadville, PA 16335
www.christianfaithpublishing.com

Printed in the United States of America

To Dina Jachens.
Not only one of my angels but my beautiful
companion along life's journey.
I love you.

CONTENTS

PREFACE

It has been some time now since I first felt the Holy Spirit come upon me and call for me to write this book. I have thought many times before about sharing my life story and the amazing impact that Jesus has had on it, yet I never felt the call to act so much as I do now. There have been stories that I have read recently in magazines, newspapers, the Bible, and even a prayer book that have had messages that I felt were directed at me to share this story. I even recently opened a fortune cookie that had the message "What are you waiting for?"

As an adult, I have developed a close personal relationship with Jesus Christ that I consider more important than any relationship I ever had with the Catholic Church or even with Jesus through the Catholic Church, if that makes sense. This relationship leads me every day during my life, and I trust in this relationship and the love Jesus has for all of us.

Now, before you give up on this book because you think it is going to be some religious zealot spouting off the entire time, I can assure you that is not the case. In fact, I am unfortunately not an outspoken prophet of Jesus outside of my immediate family, which, as you will also learn, makes sense, given everything I keep close to the vest. This book is, in a sense, me coming out and sharing some deep and scary issues that I have kept bottled up in my life for a very long time.

Hilltop Drive allows me to share with you the many unique ups and downs of my life and how I have persevered through that ride to get my life to where it is today. As you will see in the pages ahead, I often wonder why my life has come out as successful as it has. There were times I should have gotten into serious trouble for the laws I broke; but somehow, I now believe, Jesus guided me through those periods of my life to fulfill a plan he has for me.

I feel that Jesus has a plan for all of us, and I feel the sharing in this book is a big part of my plan or my calling. Have you asked yourself what does Jesus have in store for you? What is your calling? If you don't know—and many of you don't right now—never lose faith, never give up. Perhaps reading *Hilltop Drive* will inspire you or help something come into clearer focus for you, but regardless, I encourage you to pray and persevere and you will be guided.

I bet many of you have asked yourself in the past "Wouldn't it be good to go back and live our life all over again?" The opportunity to correct all the regrets we have—playing sports, going to college, making a difference in the world we live in. With so many regrets in my past, I now try to live my life regret free and encourage my children to not have any regrets as well. Take chances, live life! Excel! While I do not want to sound like a victim, I do have many regrets in my life. While some of the regrets were tangible things I wish I would have done, others were the stupid things I did in my life that if not for Jesus looking after me, I may even have more to regret in my life than I do now.

The funny thing was at the time, I didn't know Jesus was looking after me. In hindsight, it reminds me of the story of "Footprints in the Sand." This is the story where along ones walk through life with Jesus, taking place in a walk across the sand, there are four footprints in the sand for a period of time and then suddenly there are only two. The lesson of the story is that Jesus carried the person during that troubled stretch of their life. I can relate!

I certainly do not want to change anything in my life since I realize Jesus was carrying me. My wife, my three kids, my life today are all fantastic gifts the Lord has bestowed upon me; and I certainly have no regrets about any of those things. As mentioned, I do regret some things in my life, however; and I will touch upon those in this book. As the old adage goes, "If I could do it all over again…"

Life Is Great

Like a video that plays in the deepest vault of my mind, I still see and feel all the memories of growing up in El Sobrante, California, in a yellow one-story house that was 4300 Hilltop Drive. As a child growing up in an era of no cell phones and limited television channels, going outside to play with my friends was what I always wanted to do.

From the large front window of our house, one could look out over the front yard, which was beautifully manicured with a green lawn outlined in flowers, trees, and shrubs in perfectly located positions all surrounded by a white picket fence. Just feet beyond the picket fence to the north was a small out lawn that separated what we called our front yard from Hilltop Drive—a busy street that connected most of the town of El Sobrante to Richmond to the west and Pinole to the east as well as to Interstate 80, the main freeway that flowed north toward Sacramento and south toward Oakland.

On the other side of Hilltop Drive was the entrance to a Mormon church parking lot, and to the east of the parking lot stood the sprawling church with a large grass area that sat between Hilltop Drive and the church. On the exterior of the parking lot surrounding the church were dense bushy areas, which gave the church complex a unique personal boundary. Within the church complex and wrapping its way around the physical structure of the entire church was a sidewalk that separated the church from the large grass area.

If one was looking out the large front window and turned their head slightly to the left, they would see that beyond the picket fence and out lawn on the west side of the front yard was a stop sign that sat on El Centro Road, as it intersected Hilltop Drive. If one were to walk across Hilltop Drive from El Centro Road, they would walk into an L-shaped strip mall. There were many tenants that lived in the strip mall over the course of my childhood, but the main attraction was a 7-Eleven that faced Hilltop Drive, separated only by the strip mall parking lot.

El Centro Road was south off of Hilltop Drive, and after a short hill the length of about five houses, the street plateaued for about two houses and then the remaining quarter mile of the road was directly downhill. The area from my house to the plateau on El Centro Road as well as the Mormon church and 7-Eleven is what I considered my neighborhood. In an age where parents pushed their children to go play outside, this is the backdrop of my childhood memories.

The manicured lawn at the Mormon Church was, to my friends and I, the Oakland Alameda County Coliseum during the spring, summer, and fall to represent our fascination with the local stadium that hosted our favorite baseball and football teams. Some of the greatest baseball and tackle football games never recorded took place on that manicured lawn. No serious personal injuries occurred, the only incident being the occasional line drive that broke a church window, which would promptly end the game and send all the players sprinting in different directions to avoid anyone from the church catching and identifying the culprits.

After safely reaching a nearby home of one of the players, the next hour would be spent peeking out from behind the curtains to see if anyone came out from the church looking for the person who broke their window. Of course they knew it was my friends and I, as we were the only group of kids ever playing at the church. But to us, at that time, our natural instinct was to run and avoid being caught for the fear of our parents being told they had to pay for damages, which would likely cause one or all of us to get a nasty ass whipping from our parents with the belt, which was also popular back in the day.

In late fall and what Californians call winter, the sidewalks that surrounded the church was our race track for our bikes. The parking lot was our base to fly our kites, and the bushes that surrounded the church were the perfect hiding spots for hide-and-seek or the perfect base location to play guns or war. We may not have known what took place inside this large Mormon church on a day-to-day basis, but we certainly made the most of the expansive playground its exterior made for us.

On the rare days when we didn't have enough kids to play at the church, you most likely would find me with a friend or two hanging out at 7-Eleven or shooting hoops at one of my friends' houses on El Centro Road or simply doing what boys do and being goofballs and creating mischief. This was the era when I would leave my house on a weekend morning and was gone all day with friends until I heard my mom yell "Joooooeeeey" outside our house calling me home for dinner or for whatever other reason.

If I was not out with my friends, I would be hanging out by myself in my backyard. In baseball season, I would be pitching to an imaginary strike zone on our ping-pong table that was stored securely to our backyard fence against an imaginary Reggie Jackson or Steve Garvey. During basketball season, I would be beating the Lakers with last-minute buzzer-beaters in my backyard hoop; and during football season, I was kicking field goals from El Centro Road over the electrical wire that ran above my backyard that also served as my horizontal goalpost. I had quite the imagination and a lot of dreams. A lot of dreams.

Let me introduce myself. My name is Joe—well, to be official, it is Walter Joseph Jachens. I was born on November 14, 1967, in Richmond, California, to my nineteen-year old mother Beverly and my twenty-four-year-old father Walter, who went by the nickname "Skip." I would become the oldest of four children, with my sister Tricia, brother John, and youngest brother Jim all following me.

My dad worked as a teamster warehouseman at a pipe company in Oakland, and my mom was a stay-at-home mom who also worked various part-time jobs to help support the family. My siblings and I were privileged to be able to attend catholic schools, yet our family never attended church regularly. We typically would only attend church as a family on Christmas and Easter.

My dad, who was recruited as a high school quarterback as well as being honored as a member of the All New York City high school baseball team, was very athletic and very much into sports and had me playing sports as early as age six. I was good too, making the baseball all-star team annually through the age of twelve. I also played basketball from second grade through eighth grade for my catholic school team, St. Joseph's, in the very competitive Catholic Youth Organization's Oakland Diocesan League. I loved sports and excelled in them, and I have my dad to thank for teaching and coaching me along the way.

As mentioned earlier, my dad grew up in New York—in the Bronx, to be more specific. When he graduated high school, he ended up selecting a full-ride football scholarship to New Mexico State University. However, after spending only a year there, he decided to leave school to follow in his father's footsteps and enlist in the United States Navy. It was during my dad's stint in the navy that he met a fellow mariner who happened to be my mom's oldest brother, Tom. Tom set my future dad up with my future mom, and lo and behold they ended up getting married.

My mom was raised only about a mile or so from where we lived on Hilltop Drive. My mom lived at 4824 Hilltop Drive in one of the prettiest-looking houses with the nicest-groomed yard on the whole street. Due to the close proximity of the house where my maternal grandparents, Tom and Kay Murray, still lived, I was able to develop a very strong relationship with them.

My maternal grandparents were simply fantastic people. Both were born in Ireland, met in San Francisco, and raised their children in El Sobrante. They had four children. The oldest, Julie Ann, suffered from cystic fibrosis and passed away before she turned two. My uncle Tom, mentioned earlier, and Uncle Bob followed before my mom, the youngest, was born. While I never had the privilege of meeting Julie Ann, I would see her picture at my grandparents' house and think about how difficult that must have been for my grandparents to lose a child.

Now as an adult with children, it pierces my heart to think of the pain they must have went through during that time. Something much less has broken up many marriages, but my grandparents somehow persevered through this tragedy, likely due to their tremendous Catholic faith and their close relationship they had with Jesus Christ.

Since I have known my grandfather, he has been handicapped, on crutches, from a fall from a roof years earlier. My grandmother worked for the Oakland Catholic Diocese and was a bookkeeper at several parishes, typically following one pastor, Fr. John Crumblish, as he moved from parish to parish. I spent a lot of my time with my grandparents, whether doing yard projects for my grandfather or riding to school every day with my grandmother as I attended the Catholic schools my grandmother worked at during my elementary school years.

As I mentioned earlier, our house on Hilltop Drive had a big front window. It was very common to either be looking out the window or playing in the front or back yard or at the church across the street to all of a sudden hear a honk and look toward the street to see my grandfather waving as he drove by. He never looked to his right or the left to notice if any of his grandchildren were outside, just a honk and a wave toward the house all while keeping his head looking straight forward. We used to get such a huge kick out of grandpa driving by or if we were in the house or backyard and heard the honk, knowing that he was nearby. I came to really enjoy being around my grandparents and loved them very much. They were very special people who I am so very glad were part of my life.

I was also blessed to have awesome paternal grandparents as well. My grandparents Walter and Fran were also fantastic people. My grandfather worked for the city as a painter. My grandmother was a hairstylist who was so talented, she had her own room within the Bronx salon she worked at. Due to the long distance, as a child, my relationship with my grandparents in New York was limited to periodic phone calls and their occasional visits to California every other year or so. While I loved my grandparents in New York, simply due to proximity, which prevented me to be a part of their daily lives, my relationship with my maternal grandparents was naturally closer.

As you likely are envisioning, I had a terrific life as a young child living on Hilltop Drive. I had a large family, a lot of friends, a large playground across the street, and grandparents who lived close by. Everything was, in my eyes and from my perspective, perfect. I didn't know it at the time, but Jesus would soon be carrying me in our walk across the sand.

The World Ends

I enjoyed my friends and the fun times we had on El Centro Road, but I don't want you to think everything was perfect. Sure, my friends and I had fistfights through the years. I mean who wouldn't when you spent that much time together. The important thing was that the next day, all was fine and we were back playing together like nothing ever happened.

We also caused mischief as well, of which I am not proud. We did stupid and reckless things like shoot at animals and objects with a slingshot, throw water balloons and fireworks over hedges onto cars driving on El Centro Road, and numerous other stupid and embarrassing acts that seriously could have hurt someone or caused us to get in trouble with the law if something didn't go to plan. Some might think this is typical trouble boys get into while they grow up—and maybe it is—but as I reflect back now, there were some pranks that we did that could have had serious consequences. I certainly wasn't aware at the time, but someone was thankfully watching over me. Fortunately, those childhood fights and mischief were all examples of things that would heal over time. However, I would soon learn later that not all things can be healed.

As mentioned earlier, my dad was a teamster and the sole provider for our family. As one can imagine, having a family of four and owning a house is a large responsibility for a sole provider. Yes, there was some tough times, especially when my dad's union went on strike. My mom would try and help out as much as she possibly could by working jobs at a bank or clothing store, but when my dad was on strike, it was very difficult.

For example, I remember my mom gave me a dollar and sent me to 7-Eleven one day to get bread. When I paid for the bread, the clerk told me that that dollar bill was worth more because of a special marking on it or something to that effect. The clerk then put that bill in their pocket. I went home and told my mom, and she took me back to the store and pleaded to get that dollar bill back, crying to the clerk, who initially resisted but finally gave in. I remember my mom telling the clerk that my dad was on strike and we needed every cent we could. I knew times were bad, but until this episode, I never knew things were that bad.

As a child, you find yourself immune to your parents' relationship—how they talk to each other, how they act toward each other, how they argue. These are all things you assume to be normal as that is all you have ever known of your parents. As I was growing up, I would occasionally hear my friends at school talk about their parents getting a divorce or some other family issue, and I would actually think about how glad I was that I had nothing like that to worry about. However, because of what appeared to be a lot of divorces or other family issues in my community of friends, I was very sensitive to any notion of divorce within my family, and I got in the habit of always asking my parents, "Are you getting a divorce, are you getting a divorce?" "No, no, no" was always the response.

One day, however, when I was twelve, I was walking past my parents' bedroom and actually heard my dad calmly say to my mom, "What about the kids?" Curious as ever, I sat by my parents' door and listened for more details. From what I could gather, they were talking about how they were going to properly handle a separation. A separation! As I mentioned, having my parents get divorced was one of my biggest fears as a kid. I saw my friends' parents get divorced and witnessed how life drastically changed for them.

When I heard this, I immediately ran into Mom and Dad's room, crying. "What do you mean 'what about the kids? You are both liars! I thought you said you were never getting a divorce?" I just remember how upset everyone was, and my dad just held me tight, hugging me.

Just like I feared, my parents were planning on getting a divorce. My content life now ruined, my community destroyed. I remember that whole time period from that point in time to the time the separation took place was difficult. I can recall events, like various scenes from a movie, that occurred during that time. Scenes like when Mom and Dad got into an argument and Dad ran into the bathroom and locked himself in and led us to believe that he took some pills with him that he had got from Mom's brother Bob, who, at that point in time, would have had such pills.

When I heard that, I ran outside into the backyard and instead of shooting a game-winning basket, kicking a last-second field goal, or striking out a legend to win a baseball game—which I had done dozens of time in this location before—this time, I faced reality. I ran to the bathroom window and started beating on the window to break it, and I did, to prevent him from doing what I thought he was doing.

My mind quickly fast-forwards to another scene where this time Mom was going to leave in the car and Dad ran outside, and as she was trying to get into the car, Dad was trying to hug her and kiss her and definitely trying to work things out but couldn't convince Mom to stay. It was just so very hard.

I also ran away from home during this time as I was just exhausted, upset, and confused about what was going on at home. I vividly remember walking out my front door and looking back at my front window and saw Tricia, John, and Jim just looking at me, not fully understanding everything going on. I ran away to my grandparent's house and hid behind my grandpa's old Chevy that had been parked along the side of their house for some time. I really hadn't thought this out for the long term, but I was content to hide out for as long as I could. I am sure I was just looking for some much-needed attention.

On occasion, I would peek out from behind the Chevy; and on one of those times that I did, a few hours after first hiding behind the car, my grandma turned into the driveway by the Chevy and saw me. Come to find out my grandma came home early from work to help look for me, as did my dad. I remember the yelling and screaming that took place at my grandparent's house once my mom and dad made it there after I was found. It seemed like everyone was yelling at everybody, everyone so emotionally drained from this separation period, and all of us coming to the sad realization that there was not going to be any saving of this marriage.

When the separation eventually took place—and since I was the oldest—my parents asked me who I wanted to stay with, and I chose my dad. One of the things that made me want to stay with my dad was seeing the trauma my dad was going through and that my mom was getting three of the kids. This period was such a very difficult time. My mom and my siblings ended up staying in the house, and my dad and I moved into an apartment in a complex across from the El Sobrante Boys Club, about a mile away from my real home at 4300 Hilltop Drive. Just like that, I was no longer living in my neighborhood. My life had drastically changed, and to be honest, I really didn't know how to handle it.

Just before I moved with my dad into our new apartment, my parents sent me to visit my grandparents in Yonkers, New York, for the summer. While I was excited to visit them and have this awesome summer experience, I knew the real reason I was being shipped out of El Sobrante was that I was the oldest and most vocal child in the middle of this nasty split. It would be easier if I were not around, and I knew it.

That summer, my grandparents treated me to a memorable summer of fun where I met and visited with extended family members and also toured and enjoyed the sights of New York City. It truly was a great visit, and I got to know my grandparents really well.

While my visit to New York took my mind away from the many issues back in California, when I came home, it was an immediate return to reality. From the point we moved out of our house started a period of time where I was really isolated from the rest of my siblings and was really by myself. I got into a routine that started by going to school, coming home, doing homework, and then being ready by 5:00 p.m. when my dad came home so we could go to baseball practice. This was pretty much my new life. No more playing in the neighborhood until I heard my mom yell "Joooooeeeey" because dinner was ready, no more hearing the honk as my grandfather drove by the house, and no more last-second victories in my backyard. Things were now very different, much like my friends told me they were like when their parents got a divorce.

To make matters worse, during this time, my mom started publicly dating a family friend, Gary. Gary was actually a friend of my dad's, someone who coached pony baseball like my dad and would come over the house from time to time to visit. I liked Gary as he was always chatting sports with me, seemed interested in my thoughts of who might win an upcoming game, and seemed to be a good friend to my dad. That all changed, however, after he started dating my mom.

I remember, soon after they started dating, Gary started taking my mom and my siblings to movies. I found this interesting as one of the complaints I heard my mom say to my dad over the past few years was that he never took her anywhere. Not out on dates, not on vacations, nowhere. Now, here is Gary taking my mom and my siblings to the movies regularly. This would only grow my anger toward my mom and Gary, and it escalated into a regrettable scene.

One day, soon after they started dating, Gary was at one of my baseball games with my mom. I was absolutely pissed to see them together while I was out in the field. I also felt so bad for my dad, who was coaching my team. Everyone in the baseball league knew Gary and my dad, and now Gary was dating my mom. I was embarrassed being around anyone from baseball and could only imagine how my dad felt. It was absolutely horrible, and I was so angry.

After the game, my mom and Gary came up to me as I was walking off the field, and I immediately told Gary to essentially "go to hell." This was totally an abnormal behavior for me, but I was so torn up. I knew they were trying to reach out to me since I had been excluded by them since the breakup, but I absolutely hated my mom dating Gary, and I let him know it.

Shortly thereafter, the divorce was finalized, and my mom and Gary soon married. Not long thereafter, my mom gave birth to a child; and just like that, our family was officially no more. My mom and Gary had a daughter, Angela, who I should state has become someone I view as not my half sister but my sister. She has grown into an awesome person whom I love and who came into this ordeal by no fault of her own.

Life seemingly went on for everyone involved. For me, that meant when I wasn't playing baseball, I hung out at the boys' club a lot, which was a good thing. The boys' club was now my new outlet for entertainment across the street. On a personal note, however, outside of life at the boys' club, I had started to notice that I was becoming angrier quicker and easier now, and I often took it out on the one and only person I felt that was there for me at the time—my dad.

I would get pissed at my dad at baseball practice as I thought, for some reason, he was picking on me or simply for no good reason at all; and I would run away from practice, during the middle of practice. My dad would have to leave practice to go drive around the area surrounding the practice field and find me. I think I just started to feel the weight of the whole situation that had transpired over the past year, and my dad was the only one there, so I took out my frustration on him.

Don't get me wrong, my dad and I did bond over this as well. One example I remember is sitting in the living room of our apartment with my dad one night and I started crying and telling him how much I miss Mom, and he just kind of hugged me. He isn't a real emotional type of person but said that he did too, and that was a moment I will never forget.

I do think if I didn't have the boys' club available to me, the stress would have been somehow worse. It truly became my second home and a place where I could go and shoot hoops or play ping-pong and just forget about everything else. I was just becoming a teenager, missing my mom and my siblings and wondering if they were thinking about me. I would think this would be a hard thing to understand even as an adult, much less the thirteen-year-old I was at the time.

After my mom married Gary, they and my siblings all moved into Gary's house, which was in San Pablo, about three miles away from our house on Hilltop Drive. After they moved out, my dad and I subsequently moved back into the house. Suddenly our once-bustling family home on Hilltop Drive seemed very large as the residency dropped from six to two. Moving into our house, however, allowed me to be closer to my friends on El Centro Road again. Being with them, playing sports at the church or just hanging out, helped me pass the time; and like all things, time supposedly heals all wounds. Or does it?

My dad soon started dating a few women as well. He was playing on a coed softball team and started seeing one of the women on that team. After that relationship ended, he started dating a woman from his work. I remember he brought her home one night after work, and we went to the Hilltop Mall together. This may sound weird, but I really became unsettled when my dad bought this woman a new pair of jeans that night. I felt this way for two reasons. First, I was not used to my dad or my mom spending money for wants versus needs. We weren't poor but we weren't rich, and I felt my mom and dad spent their money wisely. To see my dad act differently in an apparent attempt to impress, scared me. At that moment, I also started to miss my mom. The hate I was regularly feeling swept away due to a pair of Levi's my dad bought this woman, this stranger. Hard to explain my emotions, just sharing what I felt.

It got worse for me later that night. I had gone to bed, and my bedroom door was cracked open. Through the crack I could see this woman taking off her bra and moving toward the couch. I started crying—no, wailing—calling out for my dad to come to my bedroom. Yes, I was thirteen years old acting like a five year old. At the time, I did not realize why I was acting out like I did, but I am sure seeing the physical proof that my parents were not ever getting back together triggered something in me. Looking back on that night, I am so embarrassed and feel really bad that I ruined that night for my dad.

Although ever the optimist, I eventually realized my mom and dad were not going to get back together. Russ Gordon, our neighbor who lived directly across the street from us on El Centro Road, was one of my dad's friends. My dad and I would regularly hang out at his house with him and his girlfriend, Cheryl. Russ eventually set up my dad with his cousin, Cheri, and they soon started to date regularly and became serious pretty quickly.

Cheri lived in Antioch, which was over thirty miles east of El Sobrante. As time went on, I found myself spending more time at home alone as my dad spent time with Cheri. Not long thereafter, my dad let me know that we were going to be selling the house and moving into Cheri's house in Antioch. While I knew this was a possibility because they were dating, this was not something I was a fan of. Moving again? This time to a new city? I was a very pissed off thirteen-year-old eighth grader who just wanted to go back to the days of my mom and dad and my brothers and sister living together at 4300 Hilltop Drive.

I need you to stick with me for the next several paragraphs. As promised, this is not propaganda or prophecy but simply my understanding of life that I feel is important for you know as you continue to read my life's story. I think knowing this will help you know the place I am coming from.

So I think everyone has a different view of what happens when you die. Some believe the good go to heaven and the bad go to hell for eternity. Some believe in reincarnation; some don't believe at all. Earlier in my life, I was really scared of death, so I always had this unrelenting curiosity during my life to understand what happens to us when we die.

This curiosity has led me to read and become attached in a way to stories of near-death experiences. From my reading, I have to come to believe that when we die, the good go to heaven and the bad go to hell. The souls that go to heaven are reunited with Jesus, God, loved ones who are still in heaven, saints, and angels. I believe that there are many stages a soul has to climb as part of their journey, and that means there are tasks and challenges that each soul will face in each of their life stints, meaning the soul is only in heaven for a period of time before being placed again into a new fetus to start their next journey. Trust me when I tell you I am surprised as anyone to have come to believe in reincarnation. I laughed this notion off as a younger Catholic, but this is truly now what I believe.

This belief that I have formed is certainly not that of the Catholic Church but one that does still have Jesus and his Father as the head of the heavenly kingdom. It saddens me as I feel that some of my relatives in heaven, some I have met and others that I have not met on earth, will not be there when I am there. They may have been already placed into a new life here on earth. For example, my son Jordan was born and raised in Michigan but has had this unique connection to New York City ever since he was a small child. In addition to unexpectedly starting to root for my grandfather Walt's favorite baseball team, the Mets, at a young age, he has said several things throughout his life that I have openly questioned if his soul and my grandfather's are the same. Not that it matters, but that is the process I believe souls go through. What I am trying to say is, there is a chance I may not meet some of the souls from my family.

On the flip side of this is that there are specific learnings each life has for that soul to experience, endure, and conquer during each lifetime. I believe these are laid out for us by Jesus, and it is our journey of life. Of course, it has taken me fifty years to come to formulate my belief, so it is natural for a thirteen-year-old to wonder why he was being forced to go through this disruptive divorce period and move to Antioch. In hindsight, I now see this as my first major challenge in my journey of this life.

Home Away from Home

Whenit came time to organizing a neighborhood football game in an era without cell phones, a few of us would split up the responsibility of going to all of our neighborhood friends' homes to see if they were available to play. For instance, one of our friends would go to the homes of our friends on El Centro Road; others would go to the neighboring street of Santa Maria or Alhambra to round up some kids to play. It took time, but eventually everyone who was able would show up at the church for the football game we were planning to have. Memories from these games and time spent with these childhood friends will remain with me always.

From a young age, sports have been a big part of my life, and I wanted to share with you some special moments where sports have shaped and impacted my life. As I have already mentioned, my dad had a love for sports, having played baseball and football his entire life. My dad played on the same high school baseball team as Ed Kranepool, who went on to play on the 1969 New York Mets World Championship team. In fact, my dad, Ed, and one other high school teammate had their pictures printed in *Life* magazine together during this time. My dad received tryout offers from Major League Baseball teams but elected to pursue college football. My dad's passion with sports was a major influence in my life and became my passion as well, even at a young age.

While I have shared my struggle of mentally dealing with divorce at a young age, I also want to talk about how important sports were in my life during this time and how it really helped me get through this difficult period. While I played basketball and baseball as a young boy, I also became a very big sports fan of our local pro sports teams in the Bay Area. I was a huge fan of the A's, the Raiders, and the Warriors and grew to know their records and their player statistics better than my schoolwork, so my parents would always tell me. In the early '80s, shortly after the divorce, I occasionally would travel by bus with the El Sobrante Boys Club to go to the "Oak-land Ala-meda Coun-ty Coli-seum," as famously announced by legendary sportscaster Howard Cosell to watch a weekday afternoon A's game. It was always a thrill for me to attend a baseball game in person.

I also had the opportunity as a young boy to watch the Warriors practice at the Coliseum Arena with my St. Joseph's boys' basketball team. Interestingly enough, Gary, who was a family friend at the time, had made the arrangements through one of his friends for our team to attend. It was a wonderful experience to see Robert Parrish, Clifford Ray, John Lucas, and others practice under the tutelage of legendary Warrior coach Al Attles. I still can remember how amazed I was by how tall the basketball players were! I had never seen people that tall before in my life. After practice, our team got to shoot around on the arena floor, and I noticed that Warrior first round rookie Ray Townsend used that time to go have a nice conversation with my mom. I remember giving my mom a hard time about Townsend trying to pick her up.

My dad was never a big NBA basketball fan. I, on the other hand, enjoyed the game and was, and still am, a big Golden State Warriors fan. I remember going to my first NBA game at the Oakland Coliseum Arena with some friends of mine when I was about eleven years old. The Warriors were hosting the Atlanta Hawks. We didn't have great seats, but the Warriors were not a very good team and thus did not draw a large crowd. Soon after the game started, my friends and I found empty seats that were just rows from the floor and sat in those for the remainder of the game.

When I got home from the Warriors game, I convinced my dad that he and I should go to a game and we can buy cheap seats and move down real close. Soon thereafter, we went to a Warriors game and bought two tickets that were essentially seats close to the Coliseum roof, so high up that the players look like ants. After the game started, I led my dad down to two empty seats that were close to the court. A few minutes later however, the usher came up to my dad and I and asked for our tickets. After explaining to the usher that we moved down to these empty seats, the usher asked us to return to our seats. My dad was embarrassed and very pissed off at me. I immediately suggested that we go find some other empty seats in other sections of the arena, but my dad would have nothing of it. We were going back to the top!

If you thought things couldn't get worse, think again. When we finally made our way back up to the roof, we found that those seats are also very popular and desired by some folks as well, believe it or not. People like to go up there and smoke pot! Yes, pot! The area around the seats my dad and I were sitting in, the ones we originally purchased, was surrounded by many young men sitting in this section smoking pot and oblivious to the game going on below. My dad gave me a look that told me he would never go to another NBA game again. I think he has remained true to that commitment.

While I never had the opportunity to go to Raiders game as a young boy, my parents did take me to special events they knew I would enjoy. I especially remember when my mom took me to see the great linebacker Jack Tatum at J. C. Penney at the Hilltop Mall. Jack signed an eight-by-ten black-and-white picture that I still have today. I also remember my parents taking me to see a charity basketball game as well as a charity softball game between some of the Raiders players and our parish men's basketball and softball teams. One very memorable moment that I had was when legendary wide receiver Cliff Branch came up to me in the crowd during the softball game and gave me some money and asked him if I could go buy him a hotdog! "Of course!" I said and ran up to the snack bar and bypassed other people in line informing them that I was buying a hot dog for Cliff Branch. When I brought the hot dog back to Cliff, he asked if I wanted a bite. I politely said no, but as one could imagine, it was a very exciting encounter with a professional athlete.

One of my fondest sports memories was in 1978, right before the divorce, when I was riding—actually, lying—in the back of our family station wagon as our family was returning home from a family outing. My dad had the 1978 World Series on the radio, and I remember listening to the final game and hearing that Bucky Dent was the World Series MVP. Everything I had heard up to that point about Dent was positive and inspiring that when I heard he won the MVP, I instantly became a New York Yankees fan and Bucky Dent became, and still is, my favorite Major League Baseball player. In June 1980, my dad took me to a twilight doubleheader at the Coliseum between the Yankees and the A's. The place was packed, and we had standing room tickets behind the left field bleachers. It was a beautiful night for baseball and a very special time for my dad and I as we watched the A's and my Bucky Dent-led Yankees split a doubleheader.

In 1981, when I spent the summer in New York with my grandparents, my grandfather surprised me one day by taking me to a White Plains, New York, mall where Yankees players Bucky Dent, Paul Blair, Bobby Brown, and coach Jeff Torborg were doing an autograph signing. What a surprise and what a thrill! I remember telling Bobby Brown that I saw him hit a home run in Oakland last season. I still have that autographed baseball.

While some of these stories are while I was younger and my parents were still married, they show the foundation of sports in my life. I enjoyed playing sports, watching sports, or just talking about sports. I read the newspaper regularly to get the latest updates and tried to collect as many baseball or football cards as I could. Sports was my hobby, and I was addicted to it. However, when my parents got divorced, it also became my sanctuary, a place I could temporarily escape the struggles I was having on a daily basis dealing with my new reality.

When my parents initially separated and I was living with my dad, my professional Oakland teams and their stadiums became somewhat of a home away from home for me and my friends. I was old enough to take Bay Area Rapid Transit (BART) by myself from Richmond to the Coliseum to see the A's. The best way to say it is that I explored the Oakland Coliseum. I became so intrigued about the stadium and wanted to see every bit of it that I could. My friends and I would start every game off by going to the players' parking lot and waiting for the visiting team to get dropped off and walk by us as they headed into their locker room. Then it was off to batting practice to see if we could get a ball. During the game, we roamed the stadium trying to get a look at the field from every possible angle.

After the game, we often stuck around the stadium to see what people left behind. One game we actually walked into the dugouts of both teams. In the A's dugout, still taped to the wall was the original lineup card that Billy Martin, the A's manager at the time, had written for the game that day. I took the lineup card but unfortunately have lost that over time. Another time, from what we could see, my friend and I realized that we appeared to be the only two people left in the stadium following an A's weekday afternoon baseball game. We thought it would be fun to see if we could go up into the press box and check out the view from there. When we got to the second level and to the door that led into the press box, we figured it would be locked. On this day, however, we were in luck.

The main press box door was unlocked, and as we opened it slowly and peeked in, we found the place to be deserted. Throughout the entire press box were game sheets given to select fans and media about the upcoming game, scattered about. I most vividly remember finding the soda dispenser in the press box and pushing on the Coke tap to see if it still worked. It did! I put my head under the tap and let the Coke flow! Life at that moment was very good! A brief distraction from reality.

After filling up on soda, I saw a red phone on the desk and thought it would be cool to call my dad and tell him where I was calling him from. I dialed my home number, and my dad answered. As I started to talk to him, telling him where I was calling him from, I kept hearing him say, "Hello, hello." He couldn't hear me! I hung up and redialed, and the same thing happened. It was a one-way phone, which I still am not sure of its purpose.

Sometime after my mom and dad separated, one of my friend's single mom started spending more time around our house. Sonny was a very nice lady, and one could tell she had a thing for my dad. My dad befriended her, but I think that is as far as it went. Sonny worked for carmaker Datsun, and at the time they were a big sponsor of the Oakland Raiders. As a result, Sonny was able to get Raider tickets, and soon my Dad and I were essentially season-ticket holders going to most home games with Sonny and her son, my friend, Bobby.

If you have never been to a Raider game, it is something that one needs to do once in their lifetime. Back in the early '80s, when I went, the crowd was insane and fans were getting in to fights throughout the entire game. For me, the best part was, of course, roaming the stadium and trying to be in the right place at the right time. That usually meant being behind the right goalpost for extra points and short field goals during both pregame and the game. The field-goal nets were lower then, and the balls would routinely go over the nets and into the stands where the fans would mob each other and wrestle vigorously to get the prized souvenir.

Another fun part of going to the Raider games was the pre- and postgame tailgating that we did. Before the game, Bobby and I would throw the football around in the parking lot while our parents and others drank a few cold ones and socialized. After the game, our parents and friends did the same, but Bobby had a surprise for me. After the first game that I went to with Bobby had finished, he told me to come quickly with him. We ran out to his mom's car in the parking lot and grabbed a cold beer out of the cooler. Bobby then started running toward the stadium toward an area outside an exit-only door where a large crowd had gathered. Bobby, with me following curiously behind, pushed his way through the crowd to get to the main attraction.

"Here you go, Tooz," Bobby hollered out.

"Bobby! Thanks, man!" hollered back the gigantic, ever-popular Raider John Matuszak. I was stunned! Bobby knew John

Matuszak? He brought beer to John Matuszak? Sure enough, while I am not sure how it started, it had become a postgame ritual for Bobby and John. Every week John would sign postgame autographs until everyone who waited for one had one. I remember John telling the crowd, "You guys spend your money and time to come out here and support me, the least I can do is stay out here and sign autographs for everyone." I became a big fan of the Tooz and respected him very much for what he did each week for the fans. Tooz was a class act, and I was saddened to hear that he died at age thirty-eight in 1989 due to what was largely speculated to be caused by a life of hard partying.

With Sonny and Bobby, my dad and I saw many Raider games, but the one that I remember most was my first Monday Night Football game at the Oakland Coliseum. The Raiders were playing their rivals, the Pittsburgh Steelers. I remember two things from this night. One, the crowd was even crazier than it typically is for Sunday games, which I never thought was possible. Second, I remember Terry Bradshaw, the Steelers quarterback, getting hurt in this game and lying on the field and the crowd was applauding and going crazy because we hurt their star! I remember being stunned that even the rough and violent Oakland crowd would stoop so low as to loudly cheer a player being injured.

The next year, the Raiders would pack up and move to Los Angeles, and myself and thousands of other Raider fans were truly pissed off at owner Al Davis for leaving town. My dad and I were so angry that we immediately switched our allegiance to the San Francisco 49ers, the other Bay Area team who traditionally had been a very poor team but had made it to the playoffs that season. If there was any doubt in my mind that I had made the right move to root for the 49ers, it was confirmed when Dwight Clark made "the catch" to beat the Dallas Cowboys in the 1981 NFC Championship game and send the 49ers to their first Super Bowl where they beat the Cincinnati Bengals. Even though present day the Raiders are back in Oakland, I despise them and always will for what they did to their fans and the city of Oakland in the early '80s. Still to this day, I remain a very loyal and diehard 49er fan.

After the Raiders moved, Sonny, Bobby, my dad, and I started going to a lot of A's games together. Sonny, my dad, and their friends still continued their tradition of pre- and postgame tailgating that they routinely did for football games. The A's were my area of expertise, and I got to show Bobby around. In fact, we explored the stadium even further than before together.

Bobby and I had become regulars at the players' parking lot entryway, and one night following a game, we managed to get past security and into the lower-level warehouse area that was between the Coliseum and the Coliseum Arena. As we entered the warehouse area, we could hear voices nearby and decided to hop on the elevator that was near the entryway. We pushed the elevator button and nervously waited for the elevator to come to our floor and hoped no one would be coming out.

The elevator finally arrived, the doors opened, and it was empty. We selected a floor and headed upward. When the doors opened, Bobby and I were in a long hallway. Quickly, we exited the elevator, and we went down another hallway that was connected to the long main hallway. As soon as we turned the corner, there was a room full of baseball equipment. Oakland A's catcher masks and batting helmets, bats, and other items packed this room. Bobby and I were on cloud nine. We also started to discuss our situation. Should we take anything? What if we get caught?

Bobby and I then spied a stack of a dozen or so boxes of baseballs. It was decided that we would take a baseball and split. However, when we opened the top box up, we found that all the balls in that box were signed; and after taking a quick glance, it was signed by many different major league players from many different teams. Bobby and I each took a ball and quickly exited the room.

Bobby and I then decided to further explore and took a right out of the room, opposite of the way we entered it. Bobby and I heard voices, and as we quietly walked through the hallway, we passed a room where there were two batboys talking and straightening up gear. We quietly walked past that room and out a door that led us to the area right behind home plate. I can still remember the sight. All the stadium lights were out, and Bobby and I were standing on the field behind home plate looking out onto the playing field. What a rush I felt as I stood there silently with Bobby just appreciating the moment.

As we worked our way back toward the elevator, we were seen by one of the batboys who asked if he could help us. I quickly just stated, "Where is the elevator?"

"Just down the hall," the batboy said with a weird look on his face as if he was wondering what the hell we were doing in there to begin with.

As Bobby and I exited the elevator, we ran—no, we sprinted—out of the warehouse and straight to our parents who were still having a good time tailgating. While out of breath, we still managed to excitedly tell our tale to our parents and their friends. It was truly an amazing adventure.

Sports are important to me, and like a good friend, they were there when I needed them most. It became a terrific distraction from everything else going on in my life and during those precious moments made me almost feel like I was living in a different, positive reality. I am so thankful for those experiences.

Taking Punches

When I was young, life was good. It was a happy time. It was a time of innocence. In a time with no internet and limited TV channels, the only source of local news we received was from *The Independent* newspaper which was delivered to our house every day. During baseball season, I would eagerly want to review the sports section to see the latest article from our last pony baseball game; but other than, with limited connection to the outside world, we never heard much about evil in the world like we seem to get on a minute-by-minute basis today. Perhaps that made me naïve; perhaps it had no effect on me at all. Regardless, as I reached my high school years, I would learn more about evil than I ever cared to know about.

For as long as I could remember, I always wanted to go to Salesian High School in Richmond, California. Salesian was an all-boys school, and it was a natural transition for Catholic elementary school boys in the area to graduate to. There was only one problem for me, however, and that was the tuition. It was steep, and given that things were very tight financially with my dad paying child support for three children as well as paying the mortgage on the Hilltop Drive house we lived in, having funds left over to pay tuition for high school simply wasn't there.

Heck, I remember even our food situation at home during this time was interesting. My dad would cook up all kinds of crazy things, all not expensive, but food that was different and fun to eat like egg foo young, eggplant or banana pancakes that would go along with our normal bologna, liverwurst, or olive loaf sandwiches for lunch.

So, unknown to me, my dad wrote a letter to the Salesian High School administration informing them of his financial situation and my desire to attend their school. Afterward, I did get to read the letter, and I remember thinking that all the emotions portrayed in that letter were things I never heard my dad say about me. I was incredibly flattered and thankful that he wrote this letter for me and ecstatic when I found I was accepted on scholarship to Salesian High School.

To attend high school at Salesian, I would have to take the public AC Transit bus from my home in El Sobrante to and from Salesian, in Richmond, each day as I would no longer be going to the same Catholic parish that my grandmother worked at and thus did not have a ride to school each day like previous years. However, it wasn't that long of a ride and the bus stop was right across the street from my house on Hilltop Drive.

I was so excited to be attending Salesian High School. Salesian had a great sports legacy, especially in football, and I was looking forward to becoming a part of it. When my freshman year of high school started, I was enjoying it very much. I went out for the freshman football team in the fall. My first week of tryouts went great! I was trying out for quarterback and was throwing the ball very well. I remember coming home from school that week and excitedly telling my dad how good I was doing at quarterback. I could really tell my dad was excited that I might be a quarterback, just like he was in high school.

The next week, however, brought the return of two freshman football players who had just finished their Pop Warner football season. One was a very flashy quarterback, and the other was a stocky running back, both of whom had great previous relationships playing for the head and assistant coaches. Just like that, without notice, my chances of playing quarterback were gone.

Fortunately, I did not give up and I worked hard to impress the coaches that I could hit hard and tackle well, and I was battling to become the starting inside linebacker. On the day of our very first game, our team was warming up when the Berkley High School team bus pulled up and their players exited the bus. This team had big, tall kids that were exiting the bus, and while our team stopped to watch them exit the bus, I said, "Wow, they're big!"

The assistant coach, who was standing next to me, went crazy after hearing me say that, yelling and screaming at me about being intimidated. As a result, I would not be playing that day. Of course, now I realize he was making an example out of me, but the embarrassment I felt at that moment was indescribable. As I stood there and watched our team get killed by Berkley that day, I decided that I wasn't coming back. I was done with this football team. To this day, I am not sure if it was the embarrassment that drove me away from playing or the fact that I had enough of the coaches. If I had to guess, though, it was the former.

I stopped going to practice, and when teammates would see me at school and ask why I wasn't at practice, I would lie and say I had plans or I was sick. After a while, they knew I just quit! Quitting that team is one of the things I most regret in my life.

While my self-esteem was shot and I would not try out to play any more sports at Salesian, including my beloved baseball, I did not want to leave Salesian when my dad and I moved to Antioch after my freshman year of high school. Even though I had never recovered from the embarrassment on the football field, I did not want to leave Salesian High School and my friends and go to Antioch High School, a public school, even though Salesian was now about thirty-five miles away. My dad said if I could figure out how to make the transportation work, I could continue to attend school there.

To attend Salesian from Antioch each day, I would leave the house very early in the morning and walk about four blocks to the bus stop. I would take the AC Transit bus about fifteen miles to Concord where I would get on a BART train and ride that twenty-two miles into Oakland, transfer trains, and then take that train twelve miles to Richmond at which point I would get on another

AC Transit bus and take that several miles to the nearest bus stop to Salesian High School. This was my routine to get to school and my routine coming home from school. It took about two hours each way, and thus I would arrive home around 5:00 p.m. each school day. I completed this trek to and from school my entire sophomore year.

It was hard adjusting to living in my new community of Antioch as well as the new dynamic of my dad and Cheri now living together. I honestly felt like I was in the way of their relationship. They were growing closer to each other, and I was the kid who came along—or, at least, that is what I felt. On the flip side, it took a little while, especially since I didn't go to school there, but I made a couple of friends who lived in the blocks surrounding the court that Cheri's house sat on. I even decided to play Babe Ruth baseball in Antioch and made some friends through that experience as well. In fact, it was a relationship I would make during that baseball season that led to what is likely the most disturbing incident to ever happen to me.

When I was thirteen, I stayed the night at Jay's house. Jay was on my Antioch Babe Ruth baseball team, and we both hit it off really well. His parents were both very nice people, and he lived in a nice home. Jay also had a brother, who was probably about twenty at the time, one who I heard had been in trouble with the law before but I never knew for what.

Anyway, on this particular night, I was sleeping over at Jay's house, sleeping on his bedroom floor while Jay was sleeping in his bed. I was lying right next to the open doorway of the bedroom, which was directly down the hall from his parent's bedroom. What I remember is waking up in the middle of the night with Jay's brother on top of me, pinning me down to the ground with both legs and one of his arms, and he had his free hand in my underwear and he was stroking my penis! All I heard is him whispering, repeating, "I will kick your ass if you say a word!"

Over and over he said the same line while he had this look of sick enjoyment on his face as he continued to stroke my limp penis with his free hand. Routinely he would lift his head upward to see if there was any movement or even noise coming from his parents' room down the hall.

36

Just as fast as it happened, it stopped. Jay's brother slowly got off me and reminded me what he would do to me if I said a word to anyone, and then he left and went into his room. I don't remember if I slept much more that night or not, I just remember thinking about what I should do. I didn't know Jay or his parents that well to say anything and feared they wouldn't believe me if I did. I also didn't want to say anything to my dad or Cheri because I was embarrassed, and I wasn't sure how they would react. I felt isolated and decided, regrettably so, to not say anything. I was molested, and I didn't say a damn word!

I am still friends with Jay to this day, and reluctantly, I have never told him about this. Fortunately, I did not see much of his brother again. I wasn't sure where he was, although I had heard he had moved out. However, the brother would show up every now and then and be very friendly when he saw me, saying, "Hi, Joe!" I usually left as soon as I saw him.

I heard Jay's brother got married and had kids, and I wondered if he molested his own children—or any other children, for that matter. I never felt guilty about not saying anything, until I recently looked at the California sexual offender list and saw, lo and behold, the man who molested me, Jay's brother, on the website. I wondered whom he molested and if that ever would have happened if I would have just said something! I felt like a contributor, and I regretted that.

5

Vision of an Angel

W hen you least expect it, change can happen. One day, when I was in second grade, I was having a good time selling candy door to door in my neighborhood for a fundraiser for school. I was on Alhambra Drive when I came to a house with a short picket fence around it that had a small dog in the yard. I opened the gate and entered the yard, unafraid of the small dog and optimistic that whoever lived in the house would purchase candy from me. As I made my way down the path from the gate to the front door, I dropped the candy box I had. As I reached down to pick it up, the small dog jumped at me and bit me in the face!

Again, remembering it like it was yesterday, I left the candy where it was and turned and sprinted out of the yard, through the gate, and headed northward on Alhambra toward Hilltop Drive. Once I got to Hilltop Drive, I continued sprinting east the one block to my home on the corner of Hilltop Drive and El Centro Road, crying the entire way. When I reached my house, I entered through the back door and ran through the kitchen where my mom was visiting at the kitchen table with another neighborhood mom and ran into the bathroom. When I looked into the mirror, I found that I had a hole in my upper lip that allowed me to see straight thru to my gums and my teeth! The bleeding had subsided for the most part, but the damage looked pretty gruesome.

My mom took me to the emergency room, and the medical staff stitched up the wound. I later found out the dog that bit me was put to sleep as it had never bitten anyone before and the dog owner was scared it might bite someone again in the future. Just goes to show that you never know when that path you're on can change.

As life went on in my new hometown of Antioch, I was now living it with a terrible secret inside. I was the only one who knew what Jay's brother did to me, and that weighed heavily on me. Furthermore, the commute to Salesian every day was just becoming too much. I had decided that I would attend Antioch High School my junior year. I had made a few more friends since my move to Antioch and now felt more comfortable switching schools. At home, to be honest, I still didn't feel very welcomed. My dad and Cheri were recently married, and I just felt as though they would have preferred if there wasn't a kid around. When I would come home from school, I would spend the night in my room doing homework, eating my dinner, and working out. There were no cell phones to call or text people, so my only social life was with my friends at school or in the neighborhood.

From my perspective, my life continued like this until I started to attend Antioch High School. While I was certainly very nervous about going to a new coed high school, attending Antioch High School ended up being such a blessing. I made a lot of friends, which gave me things to do outside the house that I didn't have before. It was nice feeling like a normal teenager—going to high school football and basketball games and even school dances.

Then one day, during the fall of my senior year, my life changed forever. The greatest day of my life happened two days before the big Antioch versus Pittsburg rivalry football game. My friends and I, all nonfootball players, decided we would paint our faces with school colors for the school rally the next day. After school we headed to the Antioch Mall to get face paint, and while we were there, we stopped into the Baskin-Robbins Ice Cream store. That is when I saw her— and I can still picture that moment in my head today. As I entered the store, I immediately spotted a teenage angel working behind the counter. She was absolutely beautiful, and for some reason, I had this feeling come over me that I never had with any other girl I had seen. It was like Jesus tapping me on the shoulder and saying, *"Joe, this is the one."*

My friends and I did get the paint, and we did paint ourselves for the school rally the next day, even getting our picture on the front page of the local paper on the morning of game day Saturday. While the week of the big game was fun, Dina—as her name tag read—was really all I could think about. In the weeks to come, I approached a Baskin-Robbins coworker of hers at school to enquire about Dina. I found out Dina was a junior and was single (yes!), and I told her that I really wanted to meet Dina. Soon after, she set Dina and I up with a face to face at school, and Dina gave me her phone number. Now all I had to do was call her.

While living with my dad and Cheri in Antioch, I never liked using the phone in the house. The only phone was nonportable and was in the kitchen where it seemed as though either Cheri or my dad was always in there for something. I had already felt the lack of privacy when I talked to my mom or my grandma, but now I was going to talk to a girl? I figured my best chance of calling Dina was before Cheri got home from work, around 4:30 p.m. or 5:00 p.m. With that in mind, one day soon after Dina gave me her phone number, I gave her a call.

I will never forget the call because I remember hanging up after talking to her, thinking she must live in a bad part of town. There was a dog barking, multiple people talking in the background—I thought maybe she was actually standing outside while talking to me. With the self-inflicted pressure that I believed my dad and Cheri would only approve of me dating a person from a good family, I ended the call thinking that perhaps that was a false feeling I had when I saw her for the first time.

Fortunately, Dina and I continued to talk on the phone and at school. Based on the questions I was asking her, Dina finally got the impression that I thought she must come from a poor family and live in a bad part of town. Dina found my impression funny and explained that she actually lived in a very nice townhouse in an excellent neighborhood. To think I could have stopped pursuing her over some preconceived, conceited personal standard would have been a terrible shame. Unknowingly at the time, yet fortunate for me, Jesus eliminated that potential barrier and allowed me to finally ask Dina out on a date.

At the time of our date, I was working part time as a busboy at Wongs Chinese Restaurant in Antioch and had just purchased my first car from Cheri's dad, Bill. It was a green Datsun that I affectionately called "the Turtle." My first date with Dina would include both Wongs and the Turtle as I had asked Dina to go out to dinner with me at Wongs and then go to the drive-in movie with me. Thank goodness she said yes.

It was December 3, 1984, and when I picked Dina up that night, her father, Gary, answered the door. Gary seemed like a real nice guy and chatted with me briefly while Dina finished getting ready. He never made me feel uncomfortable, which I thought was very cool. When Dina was ready, we hopped into the Turtle and headed down the street to my place of work for dinner.

Dinner was fun, but it was also a little awkward as the people I worked with were taking peeks at us; and the waitress Delores was being extremely kind and always had that "isn't this so cute" look on her face when she would refill our soda or check on how we were doing. Soon enough, though, we were done and on our way to the drive-in.

The main feature at the drive-in that night was *A Nightmare on Elm Street*. Fortunately for me, I couldn't tell you anything about that movie. Dina and I made out the entire time. At one point, I remember looking up and noticed that the windows of the Turtle were completely fogged up. It was that hot!

When the movie ended, we went back to Dina's house. Her brother Mike was out with friends that night and her parents were out together as well. Soon after we got into the living room, Dina and I were locking lips again.

You need to know that I was not that experienced with girls. There had been only one girl I had ever made out with before, and I certainly had never had sex with a girl before. As Dina and I lay on the couch and continued to make out, my hands started to get extra frisky, and Dina would continually push them away. But nonetheless, my inexperience at this type of intimacy showed, and I climaxed in my pants! How fucking embarrassing! I tried to pretend nothing was happening when I did climax, but in the weeks to follow, I would find out from Dina that see knew what had happened. I left Dina's house feeling like a major loser, and figured with my frisky hands and my premature ejaculation, she would never want to go out with me again.

Fortunately, Dina did continue to date me. We became virtually inseparable, spending our school and afterschool time together. During school, I would walk her to her class, and we would actually make out in front of the class prior to us separating and my heading off to my class. After school, we would usually go to a park and make out some more. I started to feel very, very close to Dina.

Dina and I continued to date after I graduated high school and she became a senior. While I continue to pursue it, to Dina's credit, she did not want the relationship to become sexual for a long period of time. Ultimately, however, we did take our relationship to the next level. In my heart, I knew she was the one for me, but I unfortunately tried every which way to screw things up over the next year.

Alone Again

O ne of the nice things about having the church across the street was that even if none of my friends were available to play, I could still have a great time by myself. Whether it was flying a kite in the parking lot or timing myself as I rode my Evel Knievel two-wheel bicycle around the church sidewalk in attempts to beat my previous world record time, I could spend hours having a blast all by myself. In addition, the 7-Eleven always had an arcade game or two where I could go play *Pac-Man* or *Centipede* to kill some time. Being alone wasn't devastating as a child, but I learned it is a lot different being alone when you grow up.

The summer of 1985 was a very tough and life-changing summer for me. In May, my grandma Fran passed away from the breast cancer she had been fighting. I remember speaking to my grandma days before she passed and her telling me to have a great life. I still remember speaking to her on the phone all these years later and the sadness I felt knowing I wouldn't talk to her again. She was truly an awesome lady, and I still very much miss her.

Shortly after my grandma passed, I graduated from Antioch High School. My plan was to attend Los Medanos Community College in the fall, which was located about five miles to the west of Antioch in Pittsburg. At this point in time, I really had no idea or direction of what I wanted to do with my life. My life had not followed the course I once imagined it would, and the only thing I knew for certain at this point in my life was that I loved Dina. I knew whatever happened in my life, it would involve her, and that made me very happy.

I had been working at Longs Drug Store for a short while as well, and even though my life was so much happier with Dina in it than it was before I met her, I had convinced myself that I was unhappy living with my dad and Cheri. I had convinced myself that I was, in essence, already supporting myself anyway and was only just sleeping at Cheri's house. Cheri's birthday was July 9, and I wrote a note in her birthday card that basically stated that I felt that I have been supporting myself for a while now in that I have been buying my own clothes and that I would be looking for my own place shortly. I left the card for her, and I went out that night with Dina. When I came home, my dad and Cheri and my grandfather Jachens, who was visiting for the summer following the death of my grandmother, were waiting for me.

They basically laid into me right away.

"How could you put something like that in someone's birthday card?"

"You ruined her birthday."

I was verbally attacked by Cheri and my dad and basically told to get out of the house and that I was essentially a dumb shit and that if I wanted to support myself, then I should "go out and support myself." Even my grandfather got hot and said I really needed to go back to New York with him, but I said I knew what I wanted to do and going to New York was not it. At the end, after my dad and Cheri berated me and took my car away, since the insurance was under their name, I packed my bags and called Dina. It was after 11:00 p.m. at night. Dina was asleep but answered, and I told her that I needed to be picked up since I just got kicked out of the house. She said, "Oh right," like I was joking and hung up on me. I kept trying to call back, but she was asleep and would not answer the phone. So I grabbed as much stuff as I could carry, and I walked out of the house.

I walked toward Dina's house, walking the almost two-mile-plus distance with my bags in hand, stopping every so often because they were so heavy, finally reaching her door with tears in my eyes and luggage at my feet, and informed her that my dad had kicked me out of the house. Dina's mom and dad came downstairs and said I could stay there until things got ironed out. Thank God!

I ended up staying at Dina's house for a period of time. A short time after moving into Dina's house, my dad and Cheri actually met with Dina's parents, Estelle and Gary, to discuss the current issue. No agreement came from the meeting, and I was not allowed to go home nor did I want to. We actually ended up converting Dina's parent's garage into a bedroom, and I actually moved a waterbed in there. Things weren't so bad—or so it seemed.

I need to take you back to earlier in 1985 and what likely led up to me writing that stupid, immature note in Cheri's card to begin with. I had started taking drugs during my senior year of high school. This innocent kid who loved to fantasize about striking out his favorite superstar or making the game-winning basket was now taking illegal drugs. I never ever thought I would do drugs. Never! Why did I start? No real reason except that some of my friends were doing it and I had access to it.

My drug use was primarily on the weekends during high school, but once I eventually moved out of Dina's garage and rented an apartment with my friend Scott, things really got out of control for me. I really started acting like an asshole toward Dina as well! Why on earth would I treat someone who loved and helped me so much so horribly? There I was treating Dina like I treated my dad during the divorce. I was a real screwup!

I would easily get into arguments with Dina and even hit her a couple of times. One time I remember hitting her on the top of the head with some rolled-up school papers as she walked by me in the school hallway. I did this right in front of her friends as well. This time, there were no excuses; I was the one screwing my life up—not a divorce or a sexual abuse but by my own actions—and I had no idea why I was doing what I did.

During that time, Scott also started dealing drugs, and there were now drugs available to me all the time. Thinking back upon this time, I am reminded that at any time I could have been part of a bust by the local police, but for some reason—Jesus carrying me, perhaps—they never latched on to the people who were dealers and also my friends. In hindsight, I wonder when does Jesus just get fed up and say, "*Enough with him!*" All glory to him for not giving up on me!

As a result of doing drugs and drinking a lot, my friends and I ended up doing even stupider things. On the lighter side of those activities was routinely taking beer from the drug store Scott and I worked at. We would simply take a case or two outside with us from the warehouse when we took out the trash, and we would put it behind the dumpster. Later that night, we would go back and pick it up. Even worse, sometimes we would go into the cold box—the cold room behind where the alcohol is displayed to the public—and have a beer while we were working. I am so ashamed as I write this.

But it gets worse. One night, we felt sorry for our third roommate, Abigail, who also worked at the drug store. Scott and I always picked on her, and to try and make nice for her birthday, Scott and I decided that we would turn our little fenced-in porch on our apartment into a flower room for her. One late night, Scott and I drove to a hardware store down the street from where we lived and took lattice and potted and hanging flowers that were left outside as part of the store's display. Simply put, we stole from the hardware store. At the time, we were all giggles, we thought it was fun, like we did when we stole beer or drank on the job. Again, the Lord was looking over us as if we got caught, we could have went to prison. Again, I shudder at the thought as to how my life could have changed if not for Jesus looking over me!

Needless to say, we built Abigail her flower room, and it looked really nice—excessively nice for the apartment we were living in, to be honest. It was noticed by everyone who came into our apartment or walked behind it and saw the nice lattice attached to our porch fencing.

Knowing people who dealt drugs put me in unique situations. One situation that I was in actually caused me to realize how dangerous things had become. I was with one of my friends at the time, Nick, who brought me to his brother's house one night. I knew Nick's brother was a big drug dealer, handling quantities of drugs much larger than my friends would ever have. Nick brought me into his brother's bedroom and showed me a large crystal bowl— the size of a large salad bowl that people would use at dinner to take salad from and put onto their plate—full of methamphetamine. I have no idea how much was there, but there was enough to put someone away in prison for a long time if they were ever caught. I did not feel comfortable being in a house that had that much drugs in it. I also didn't feel comfortable with the people in the house who acted friendly but gave me the impression that they had the ability to hurt you badly if they so desired. I was not in a good place in my life!

After I had moved into the apartment with Scott and Abigail, I did start to attend college at Los Medanos Community College. However, what went from weekend partying in high school turned into daily partying, and I couldn't get my ass out of bed in the morning. As a result, I was unable to continue going to school. I had reached the low of all lows.

Days and nights at the apartment were just a big party, and when we were bored, we would do even stupider things. As an example, one time, Scott and I decided to mess around and get the phone book out and started calling tow trucks. Across from our apartment complex, there was a house with a car in the driveway, and it was obvious no one was home. A street separated this house and our apartment complex, and on the apartment complex side of the street were these large bushes. It was nine or ten at night when we started calling tow trucks to come pick up this car. Scott and I would go wait in the bushes; and then the first truck would come over the hill, about three hundred yards away, and would park in the driveway and the driver would then go knock on the door. When no one answered the door, the driver would look around and then take off. Scott and I would then go call another tow truck company and then another and then another. Every time, we would sit in the bushes and watch each different tow truck driver pull up and after finding no one home, look around and then leave. Each time, Scott and I would watch and start laughing as we pranked another driver.

Scott and I were just starting to think that no one else was going to show up when all of a sudden, we saw a tow truck coming over the hill, then another truck behind it, and then another one behind that one, and another one behind that one! We suddenly realized after the third or fourth truck came over the hill that they were coming at faster speeds, they were all together, and something just didn't seem right. They were driving right toward the bush we were hiding in! Scott and I jumped out of the bush, and as we looked back, the trucks were quickly being parked on the street. The drivers jumped out of their trucks and started running after us. Scott and I ran through the apartment complex and made it to our apartment and turned all the lights off very quickly. Scott and I both jumped into bed, throwing on our pajamas as we quickly laid down.

We were both nervous and shaking and not sure if we were going to get out of this one. A million thoughts crossed our minds— *Should we stay? Should we go out the back window?* All of a sudden, we heard voices saying "They went in here, they went in here! Call the cops!" Scott and I were freaking out even more now. Shortly after, the cops showed up and knocked on the door. We didn't answer. The cops continued knocking. Scott and I debated on what to do. We agreed we should open the door, but which one of us? Scott had drugs in the house, which added a little extra concern on his part.

I decided to go ahead and do it. I went to the door and, acting very sleepy, opened it and said *hello* in a groggy tone. The cop asked me if I tried to call a tow truck. I said no. The cop then looked at one of the tow truck drivers and asked, "Is this one of them?" The driver said, "I can't tell." The cop asked, "Did anyone come and go from this apartment in the last few minutes?" I lied and said, "A friend of ours just came through but went out the back." The cop said, "Okay," and started to walk away as did the tow truck drivers. But before I could close the door, the cop turned to me and said, "The next time you call a tow truck driver, you better need one," and then he left.

Other times Scott and I would sometimes simply get bored and just drive around to see if we could find something interesting going on. One time, after Scott just broke up with one of the many girl-friends he had during this time, we decided to go get some beer and drive around Pittsburg. Our drive this day led us to the boat ramp at the Pittsburg Marina. We sat there in Scott's relatively new truck, talking and having a couple of beers.

Scott was bragging about the power of his new truck and thought he would demonstrate by driving it onto the downward-sloped boat ramp. It was probably about 10:00 or 11:00 p.m., and thus there was nobody around. Scott drove onto the ramp and let the water get up to the tires of the truck. As he tried to put the truck—a stick shift—into reverse, the gears didn't catch and the car would plow ahead, like when you miss stepping on the clutch properly, a few feet further into the water each time.

Scott tried unsuccessfully about three times before I started to get concerned. The water was now covering the hood of the truck and was almost to the base of the front windshield. Water began seeping in the bottom of the truck doors! Scott, now very panicked and concerned, tried one more time; and we plowed into the water even deeper, water now rushing into the cab through the side windows. We both hollered to each other to bail, and we both did.

We both left the truck and swam a few strokes until we could touch the bottom with our heads above water and then we walked up the ramp to the shore. I remember looking back and seeing Scott's truck entirely in the water, for the exception of the gate of the truck bed sticking out of the water and the rear lights of the truck shining below the water.

Scott and I tried desperately to see if anyone, except for a police officer, was in the parking lot; but we couldn't find anyone. We walked to a pay phone where Scott called some friends for help, but it would be a while before they would be there. Fortunately, after he hung up the phone, a truck drove by and then stopped. The driver stepped out, amazed by the stupidity he was looking at. He fortunately was able to anchor the rear of Scott's truck and chain it to his. He easily pulled Scott's truck halfway up the ramp.

Scott opened up the driver's-side door, and water poured out of it. He finally hopped in and tried to back the truck up, and guess what? The car lunged forward again! Scott got out and told our rescuer that something must be wrong as he can't put the truck in reverse. The man got into Scott's truck, put the truck into reverse, and backed the truck right up into the parking lot on his first try. He thought we were real morons! But hey, we got the truck out and did not get in trouble, so we were feeling pretty darn good! We had a few more beers and a lot of laughs on the way home that night!

Perhaps the one night that ultimately exemplifies Jesus carrying me through this period of my life was on December 24, 1985. Scott and I were at the Sun Valley Mall in Concord doing some last-minute Christmas shopping. We were inside the Gap store on the second floor of the mall as I was looking for red Levi's 501 jeans for Dina. The Gap was right next door to Macy's at the center of the mall. In front of Macy's on the second floor was Santa Claus and a Christmas display.

All of a sudden, I heard what sounded like gunshots and saw two things happen very fast before my eyes. I saw the clerks in the store run out the back door of the store, and then as I looked out at the mall walkway at the front of the store, I could see people fleeing the mall, running toward the escalator away from the center of the mall.

Scott and I were ducking behind racks of clothing as we thought someone was shooting up the place. I was really, really scared! Then, just like that, the noise stopped, and there were no people outside the store. Scott and I went to the front of the store and peeked out. Right next to us, in front of Macy's and where Santa was at, was now just a black hole covered in thick smoke!

Scott and I ran toward the escalator and kept looking back and could not believe what we saw. Everything was gone! We kept hearing rumors of a bomb from other victims as we fled. As we drove away from the mall, there was a major traffic jam; and as we were at a standstill, we were able to ask a carful of girls, who were all upset and heading toward the mall, what had happened. They informed us that they heard that a small plane had crashed into the mall.

When we finally got home, we confirmed the girl's story. We found out that the pilot of the plane had got lost in the fog and crashed into the mall. Even after the time it took us to get home, Scott and I were very amped up on the adrenaline rush from the plane crash. We invited a couple of friends over and started to drink. After a little drinking—for some unknown, stupid reason—I got in my truck and went for a drive by myself.

It was now raining out, and as I was driving—too fast, I might add, I hit my brakes and did a 180-degree spin in the street before stopping. I remember looking around and seeing not one vehicle, especially a cop. This was a major intersection next to a freeway on ramp and not a residential street. There was no one around to either catch me or for me to possibly hurt by the actions of my driving. I remember sitting there for a brief second looking out my front window facing what should have been oncoming traffic and thinking, *Oh my God, now two things today in which I could have been seriously hurt and nothing happened. Why am I so stupid? Why hasn't anything happened to me?*

Unfortunately, it got worse. In what was perhaps the most revealing thing that happened to me that showed me Jesus was in my life and wasn't going to let me screw it up happened one night at the apartment Scott and I lived in. To tell the story in full, I need to let you know that Dina was and is the only girl I have ever made love to. Now married more than thirty years, I am extremely proud of this. This, however, was almost shattered before we even got married, but an unbelievable thing happened.

My friend Jay lived next to a family where the mom had extra-marital affairs and enjoyed having them with young men in their late teens, primarily with Jay and Scott, and she was open to having multiple partners at the same time. I would often hear Scott talking dirty to her on the phone and then leaving for a rendezvous with this woman. Jay also had intercourse with this woman many times in the past. What teenage boy—especially ones who drank, did drugs, and acted irresponsibly—would not want an older woman that they could have sex with at a given moment?

One night, Scott wanted to have this woman over the house, and he wanted him and I to both have sex with her together. Scott knew that Dina and I had been fighting—this time, much worse than ever before. I actually thought that Dina and I were finished this time. We had fought a lot in the past about many different things but always reconciled. I may have done drugs, drank, stole, but I *never* cheated on Dina. I had been asked by Scott and Jay to be with this lady in the past, and I always declined. This time, I thought Dina and I were through, though; and I told Scott I would join him this time.

The older woman showed up at our apartment, and as Scott and I had talked through beforehand, Scott brought her into the bathroom. After a few minutes of foreplay, I was to then join them. As Scott and this woman were in the bathroom, giggling and starting to have fun, I started my countdown to join them. I remember being very nervous and wondering if this was the right thing to do. After all, Dina and I *always* got back together in the past; and I somehow knew if I took this next step, it would officially be over.

As the time neared for me to enter the bathroom and join them, the doorbell rang. I remember thinking, *What the hell?* I went and answered the door, and Dina was standing there. It was like an angel had sent her at this particular time to ensure I didn't screw up my life any further. I don't remember what exactly happened after that, other than we both went outside and talked. Scott, thankfully, finished with his date alone. Even as I reflect on that night many years later, I become emotional realizing what a severe twist of fate that was.

Somehow, someway, Jesus carried me across the sand in 1985. I was at the lowest of lows, and I was a loser in life. If Jesus were not there, I don't see how I could have survived. I tried many times to put myself in a position that I either should have been arrested or even killed, not to mention how I survived this period with Dina still beside me. I often wondered why Jesus saved me, but I know now he has a path for me to follow that includes me writing this book. And while I know I must have frustrated him, he continually was there to save me and help me through this period of my life.

The Realization of the Spirit

One day I was standing on my back porch and looking westward onto El Centro Road when all of a sudden a boy, a little older than me, was on a bike coming down El Centro Road at a high rate of speed only yards from the busy El Centro Road–Hilltop Drive intersection. It became evident that his brakes on the bike weren't working as he yelled out as he neared the intersection. The bike crossed through the intersection and crashed into the bushes on the south side of the strip mall. The boy was slow to get up, but eventually he did and picked up his bike and started to walk it toward 7-Eleven.

Why did that boy survive? Hilltop Drive is a very busy road with cars always coming through that intersection at a good rate of speed, fast enough that if a vehicle were to have hit him, the chances for survival had to be small at best. Was this luck or was this part of his life path that Jesus was guiding as well, protecting him at that very moment? In hindsight, that stretch of him going down the hill out of control, blindly crossing that intersection, crashing in the bushes, and then picking himself back up—I eerily find similar to my life story, with the best part being that Jesus was guiding him along the way and keeping him safe.

Once I finally got my shit together, I realized that not only was Jesus looking over me, but he put this amazing woman in my life for a reason. For some unknown reason, she stayed by me during this period of alcohol and drug abuse. I had absolutely no doubt I was in love with her, and while Dina was still a senior in high school, I asked her to marry me. My angel said *yes*!

Like myself at the time, Dina did not have any religious background or interest, but I found her to be my guardian angel in life, taking me from my loneliness and emptiness and instilling my lost pride and faith in me. Her parents were there for me as well, not only when I needed them most but along the entire journey.

As we prepared to get married in August 1987, Dina and I needed to attend an Engaged Encounter retreat weekend hosted by the Catholic Church so we could be married in a Catholic church. Interesting enough, I still have my Engaged Encounter notebook and recently reread it. There were a couple of interesting comments in the notebook that I wrote on that May weekend that I thought were fitting to share as it pertains to this book.

At the time of engagement and even marriage, Dina and I did not regularly attend church. Over time, this changed, but interestingly enough in my notebook I wrote that I hope as a result of that weekend "it gives Dina a little pat to going to church. Possibly that could be part of our relationship. It might bring an 'element' in our lives that we need other than each other." I find this statement to be very enlightening as you will see later in this book how important the church became later in our lives.

Second, this is a quote I had written at the time that speaks for itself and reaffirms what I am writing in this book: "I don't think we would be together if God hadn't planned for us to be so." Amen to that!

As I tried to continue acting like a grown-up, I learned from a good friend of mine from El Centro Road that there was this forklift operator's job being posted in the want ads in Pittsburg. My friend applied for the job and interviewed but decided not to take the opportunity, so I decided to throw my hat in the ring. I knew nothing of forklifts—or anything mechanical, for that matter—but it paid well, and I was supposed to get married in a little over a year.

So in April 1986, while back in school attending Los Medanos, I applied for this job with WalTek, a technical contracting firm, which subsequently hired me. I found out this job does entail driving a forklift, but it really is a contractor technician position that worked in research and development at the Dow Chemical, Pittsburg, California, site. As a contract employee, I worked alongside other WalTek and Dow employees, assisting in the production of an agricultural product in a pilot plant environment. Job responsibilities included working shift work and conducting product laboratory analysis and assisting with various pilot plant operations.

The work I did as a contract employee actually turned into a one-year audition, per se, as the Dow Chemical Company hired me on as a research technician/technologist in April 1987. The year 1987 proved to be a big year in my life as not only did Dow Chemical hire me, but I also married my high school sweetheart, Dina, in August.

Dina and I wed on August 15, 1987, at St. John Vianney in Walnut Creek, California. Fr. John Crumblish, the priest for whom my grandmother worked, celebrated our mass and even sang at our wedding. It was a beautiful wedding, and the reception was equally impressive, held at a hall at Heather Farms Park, also in Walnut Creek. Following the reception, Dina and I took a limousine to a hotel in San Bruno, near San Francisco International Airport, where the next day we flew to Puerto Vallarta for our awesome honeymoon.

It's interesting to think about the age we were when we got married. We were both nineteen years old. I know my mom was nineteen when she had me as a her first child, but looking back at this as an adult, I would be so unsupportive of my kids getting married so young. I have got to believe that there were people at our wedding who were thinking our marriage would never last, just due to how young and immature we were.

Later that year, we purchased our first home together at 1112 Klengel Street in Antioch, just down the street from the Antioch High School Baseball Field. We were now married, with good jobs and our own home. Life was terrific!

When I was hired as a Dow employee, I started doing what I had done previously as a contractor; but after a few years, I moved away from shift work, and my new job responsibilities were straight days focusing on coordinating maintenance and environmental activities for the research and development area of the Pittsburg, California, site as well doing some computer programming work for one of the pilot plants on the site.

During this time, I started playing competitive slow-pitch softball both in the Antioch and Pittsburg recreational leagues but also in some industrial tournaments representing Dow. I really missed playing competitively and played multiple nights a week for league play and in tournaments on the weekend, mostly in Northern California, but we would play an annual industrial tournament in Central California at Morro Bay. Dina and many of the other spouses and girlfriends were always there to support us. It was nice, as most of the other players didn't have kids yet either, so we could go out and have a cold beer after the game and socialize. The guys I played with and their significant others were absolutely awesome people who have become lifetime friends.

Speaking of children, Dina and I were trying to have kids since we were married. Again, I am making the assumption the timing wasn't right yet with the path Jesus laid out for us. Time went on and we kept trying, so at least it was fun.

While on the topic of softball, I do want to share a story of an event that occurred when I was playing in a recreational league one night in Pittsburg. It just goes to show you never know when the next curve in your life's journey is coming.

There were two teams in our league made up of all young African American players, a black-colored team and a red-colored team. Both of these teams were very competitive and always appeared to be friendly when we played them. One night, we were playing the red team and our team was batting. I had just walked and was standing on first base when all of a sudden from the darkness of left field, you could hear a car screeching its tires very loudly. Everyone looked over the fence toward the left field foul line to see what was going on as the screeching noise grew closer. All of a sudden, a car appeared next to the third base dugout that the red team reserves were sitting in. The next thing I hear was the sound of gunfire. I didn't know it was gunfire at first, and I didn't get down until I saw everyone else doing the same.

I then heard bullets ricocheting off the fence behind where I was laying. The car then took off, and we dashed off the field; however, the car came back again. This time, I dove behind our coach— he was the biggest guy—as he was lying behind a garbage can behind the first base dugout. Again, shots were fired, and I was told later it was members of the black-shirt team in the car and that these two teams were gangs, and during the second pass the red team actually pulled guns out of their baseball bags and fired back! The car took off this time, and everyone made the run to our cars, which were actually parked across the street from the city park in the Pittsburg City Police parking lot! Think we heard or saw a cop car? Nope! I have had games called for lightning and rain and muddy fields but never for a drive-by gang shooting, until that moment.

In 1990, I took another opportunity within Dow at the Pittsburg site to become the environmental health and safety (EH&S) coordinator for a specialty monomer pilot plant at Dow in Pittsburg as well as taking on the additional responsibility as the site research block maintenance coordinator. My new responsibilities included implementing EH&S work processes in the pilot plant, which meant interacting with the plant on a daily basis on EH&S issues to interacting and communicating with the Environmental Protection Agency when they visited or inspected the plant. I also was able to chair the Site Research Safety Committee for two years, which presented me the opportunity to give several presentations to Dow management on the Pittsburg Research Block safety initiatives.

In early 1992, we thought we may finally have the gift of a child. After having so many false pregnancy tests over the past few years, we finally got a positive. Dina went in to the hospital to have a blood test to confirm the pregnancy, and we had to wait for them to call us with the results. We were on pins and needles awaiting the call. I remember it like it was yesterday when that phone finally rang and I picked it up. Dina was sitting on the couch in the living room watching and listening to me talk to the nurse on the other end of the phone. When the nurse confirmed the results and I repeated it,

Dina yelled "Yes!" from the couch; and when I got off the phone, we were hugging each other and crying with joy! We had a baby coming into this world!

When the hospital confirmed the pregnancy test, it started a duration of planning and anticipation. My first reaction was to start working on the baby's room while Dina's was to educate herself, reading pregnancy and birthing books to see what she could expect during the nine months ahead.

Halfway through the pregnancy, the doctor asked us if we wanted to know the sex of the baby. We both said no as we had made an earlier commitment to each other that we would wait until the birth and be surprised. When I initially told Dina I would wait, I had no idea how long those nine months would be. It was as if the biggest Christmas present under the tree was for you and every day you walked by and saw it and wanted so badly to see what was inside!

We patiently stood by our promise, however; and when the gift was finally opened, Dina and I received the best present anyone could ever ask for.

On September 11, 1992, about a month and a half before our baby was to be born, my grandfather Tom passed away after battling cancer. I very much loved and respected my grandfather, and I wanted to speak at his funeral. Below is what I spoke at his funeral on September 14:

> I wanted to be able to say a few important things about my grandfather that if some of you here didn't know before should know about this great man.
>
> As all of you know, my grandpa was a very strong man. As much as this man suffered, he never complained. He always was more concerned about how other people felt and how much worse off other people were than he. I remember a couple of years ago when he came home from a rehabilitation stay at the hospital and he was still in a lot of pain. The first thing

he told me was that he felt "lucky" because there were so many other people in that same hospital that were far worse off than he. He referred to the young children who had cancer or the other patients that were confined to a wheelchair. I couldn't believe this man who, weeks before our family thought would never fully recover, is not seeking our comfort, nursing, or hospitality but instead is shedding his pity on other unfortunate people.

My grandpa was my idol, and I know secretly he was some of yours. I hope to be as strong and as courageous as he was, and I know still is. I wish to have his great sense of humor, his loving nature, and, most importantly, to be able to draw in the sense of a "happy family" whenever family is around me. Every time I go to my grandparents' house, I instantly feel loved and welcomed. That is what I hope I can do for my children and grandchildren one day and that I think was one of my grandfather's greatest attributes.

My child, due in a couple of months, will never know his great-grandfather. That, to me, is the one thing I wish I could change. I know there will be many nights that I will be up late telling my child about his/her great-grandfather like most people tell their children about their idols or heroes. My child won't personally know Grandpa, but he or she will grow up knowing what a great man he was and will grow up with the same attributes as I was raised in my family that was brought down from my grandfather's family before that. In that sense, my grandfather will still live inside my child. And my child will know that.

You know, before I go on, right about now, I know Grandpa is listening to me talk to you, and

I am sure he is saying one of his many millions of quote, unquote "Grandpa" jokes as the family jokingly used to call them. If I were to guess, he is probably telling God that my mouth right now is like a 7-Eleven store. It's open twenty-four hours a day. One of his favorite sayings. In that sense, I mean I'm sure he wouldn't want anyone going on about him like I am. But the truth of the matter is, even if I am not up here, everyone here knows what a great person Grandpa was, that I am certain.

I will miss Grandpa. I will miss his humor, his intelligence, his kindness, and, most of all, the friendship we had. I will miss eating dinner with him, talking to him on the phone, and talking politics with him—we all know Grandpa and politics. We had no choice but to talk politics with Grandpa. I will miss seeing him and Grandma together. I will miss seeing him around the holidays and birthdays, but we must know this is something Grandpa would not want us to do. He would not want our holidays and birthdays spoiled by sad people tearfully remembering him. We do know that, and we do know we will all miss him.

So I would like to end this talk by going over some of the highlights that I personally shared with Grandpa and that I'll never forget.

I remember mowing his lawn, what a risk that was. He wanted it to perfection. He, I think, to this day was the toughest boss I ever had. One day, a garden snake came out on the lawn and scared the heck out of my little twelve- or thirteen-year-old body. Okay, not so little twelve- or thirteen-year-old body. Old boss Grandpa, noticing a delay in work, came striding over on his crutches and saw the snake, picked it up with his crutches, and flung it out of sight. Wow, I thought, he sure is brave, my grandpa coming over here to rid the snake while I, a teenager, am scared straight.

I remember my grandpa riding his old blue car past our house on Hilltop Drive, putting his hand out the window to wave to our house while never taking his eyes off the road. John, Jim, Tricia, and I used to look out our front window to see how many times we would see Grandpa drive by and wave. We always thought that was hilarious.

I remember my grandpa telling my beautiful wife and mother-to-be, Dina, as he lay on his deathbed that he prays for *her* and the baby all the time. Another item that goes on my "I can't believe this guy" list. Always thinking of others before himself. To sum it up, the guy you wanted to be on a sinking ship in the middle of the ocean was Grandpa.

I remember watching my grandpa's face light up when he always saw my nephew Ryan. What a kick he got out of little Ryan. Ryan—JJ, he forever nicknamed him.

I remember the pride my grandpa showed when he talked of the accomplishments his family have made. His children and grandchildren and distance relatives and longtime friends—all of us here today. He was so proud of his family, just like we were of him.

I remember buying Grandpa a lottery ticket after lottery ticket after lottery ticket after lottery ticket. I remember the rest of the family buying Grandpa a lottery ticket after lottery ticket after lottery ticket after lottery ticket with no success.

I honestly thought for sure he would end up on *The Big Spin*. That would have been so fitting. He was a perfect fit for that show. But you know what, he did win the lottery, the grandest prize of all. He, not us, is in heaven right now looking down on the poor world he just left. I think about it, and you should too. Don't you think he is in a better position than us? Up there?

So maybe we should only be sad about Grandpa leaving this earth but rejoice for the fact that he is in heaven, which I am sure is a far greater place than where we are now and, as of last Friday, a far greater place now than it was on last Thursday, now that they have our grandpa up there with them.

I love you, Grandpa!

I took so much comfort in how my grandma responded to my eulogy. She was so proud of it that she made a beautiful print of it and framed it in her home. I was so happy I could contribute on that day.

Toward the end of the pregnancy term, we joined a Lamaze class. This not only helped educate us but really helped pass the time, slowing down the expectation of what was only weeks away now. We would always remember this Lamaze class because two hours after we left our last class, five days before our baby's due date, Dina went into labor.

When we arrived at the hospital, the nurse confirmed that this was the real thing and it also wasn't going to be that long of a wait. The event we had been waiting so long for was about to happen. Our present was about to be opened—or so we thought.

Dina remained in labor for about five hours and had been pushing for a while when the doctor returned to the newly decorated birthing room. "You've been pushing for two hours, and we still have had no success. I'd like to do a cesarean," the doctor announced.

"Please just take this baby out of me," Dina cried out.

I was sitting next to Dina, holding her hand, and I started to cry, knowing how badly Dina wanted to have the child naturally.

After being wheeled into a dark, unattractive operating room, I sat next to Dina, talking to her as both of us were shielded from the surgery taking place by a big green drop cloth that hung above Dina's chest. What seemed like a lifetime longer but actually was only fifteen or twenty minutes, the doctor told me to stand and watch as the baby was about to be lifted from Dina's womb. I stood, nervous but extremely excited, and the doctor lifted out the baby and yelled, "It's a girl!"

Experiencing the birth of my child, whom we named Megan Jennie, was the most fascinating thing I have ever seen. Not only did it produce the most beautiful baby in the world, but it culminated a special period in the lives of both Dina and myself. The birth itself took only minutes in comparison to the long preparation period that preceded it. Needless to say, it was worth the wait to open up that Christmas present.

I love Dina more today than in any time in my life. She is an amazing wife and mother, and I am even more thankful today that Jesus and Dina didn't give up on me when it would have been understandable to do so.

8

The Yellow Brick Road

I often wondered how many balls the Mormon church maintenance folks found when they trimmed their bushes or pruned their trees or cleaned the gutters on their roof. We lost a lot of balls at that church. Footballs, baseballs, kickballs, tennis balls—we lost them all. We were always hoping that when they found these lost items, they would leave them outside for us, but they never did. In fact, I don't think they wanted us playing on their grass or on their sidewalks altogether. I guess I can't blame them. We did break some windows, and I am sure we caused divots in their lawn and created black brake marks from our bicycles on their sidewalks. In hindsight, they were very kind to let us use and enjoy their property. There were not any nearby parks, so if we were to ever get booted from the church, we had nowhere to go.

In early January 1994, the employees at the Dow Pittsburg site were told by Dow management that the Pittsburg pilot plant facility was shutting down. It was a surprise to all employees at the Pittsburg site, especially myself, since I worked in the pilot plant facility. All of a sudden, my job position had been pulled out from under my feet.

Within the next couple of weeks, my supervisor approached me and told me there was an opportunity for me with Dow in Midland, Michigan. At first, I was stunned. In my seven years with the Dow, I had never visited the company's headquarters in Midland, Michigan. The only feedback I ever received were from coworkers who visited Midland for training classes or special meetings. I would be dishonest if I said their feedback made me want to move to such a place. The responses I usually heard were "It's freaking cold there!" by winter visitors or "There's nothing to do there. It's in the middle of nowhere!" by spring and summer visitors. I had even often referred to Midland as Oz, comparing it to the movie where all roads lead to this magical city that one only hears about and has never seen.

A couple of days later, I reached out to my supervisor to help me understand what other options I had. My supervisor and I had a very profound discussion that day and I learned that I had an option to stay in Pittsburg if I wanted a lab technician role in an agricultural facility. At the end of the conversation, he stated, "It really comes down to this. You have to decide what you want to do with your life. You can either work with your hands or work with your mind."

His example was very eye-opening to me. He was telling me I could take a chance and move to Midland and be a decision-maker for Dow or I could stay in Pittsburg and work in a lab or in a manufacturing facility in the type of role I am currently in. He wasn't being derogatory to either role, just using that example to illustrate how he saw the opportunities in front of me. The interesting thing was, I felt I could be a good people leader one day, if I ever were to reach the ranks of such a role, so that decision-maker comment resonated with me.

This decision-making process moved very rapidly. There were two other people with whom I worked who were in similar positions to me—going back to school (which I had started again) and striving for something more than what they were currently doing for the company. One of those coworkers declined the opportunity, but another had already accepted a salaried position with Dow in Dalton, Georgia.

Following my meeting with my supervisor, he set up a meeting for me with the R&D director. We had a great conversation during which I explained to her my desire to complete my education and eventually have a salaried position within Dow. She also seemed pleased with our discussion and subsequently setup an interview for me in Midland, Michigan.

I arrived in Midland on Super Bowl Sunday 1994, and as I landed at the Midland Bay Saginaw International Airport, all I could see was snow. It was everywhere! After departing the plane, I stepped outside the terminal to look for my rental car. It was freezing outside! I was already wondering if I had made the right choice. What was I doing in Midland, Michigan?

However, as I drove on the slick, icy road to the hotel, the sun broke through the clouds and glistened off the snowpack. It was a beautiful sight. It would be just the start of good things to come from this trip.

When I got to the hotel in Midland, the Bills and Cowboys were playing in the Super Bowl; and I planned to just stay in and watch the game in my room. I did notice—and this is how naïve I am—that there was a tornado evacuation placard on the back of the hotel room door. I was curious as I never experienced a tornado before and really had no idea as to what triggered a tornado or if they could occur in the winter or not. Of course, later that night, the hotel siren went off, and I took off out of the hotel room quickly, making my way down the emergency stairway to the frigid, snowy outdoors in my shorts! You would be right if you guessed my first thought was that there was a tornado. Actually, it was just a false fire alarm. Looking back at this now, I laugh at this story for absolutely how clueless I was about tornados.

I interviewed the next day with several people who worked in Dow's pharmaceutical pilot plant in Midland. One of the people I interviewed with was a young chemical engineer, Mark, whom I knew from his time working at Dow's Pittsburg facility. I had even played against Mark in softball a few times. It was nice to see a familiar face.

Mark basically told me that he understood that if I wanted this position, it would be mine and the interviews that day was more of a formality to get to know me and ensure no one there had any red flags. This news was a relief for me as I now knew this decision was mine now to make. I just needed to somehow convince Dina that she would enjoy living here.

Upon my return to Midland, I found Dina to be incredibly supportive of us taking this opportunity—or adventure, as we called it. We soon decided that we were both young and if things just didn't work out, we would move back to California and start over again. With that decision made, I accepted the job, and we put our house up for sale and prepared for the upcoming cross-country drive with little Megan.

During the four-month stretch between the time I accepted the role and the time I started in early May, so much happened in my life. First, Dina and I found out she was pregnant with our second child! It was both so strange and exciting to think this baby would be born in Michigan. It was also so neat to think that Megan would now be a big sister!

Second, as part of the deal for this transfer, Dow would pay for my moving costs; but I was responsible to sell my home. We prepared the house for sale, but we did not get any offers and decided to rent out the home. Our good friends Rick and Julie said they would manage the property for us in our absence, which was a true blessing. While we desperately wanted to sell the house before we left, this was unfortunately the situation we were forced to deal with.

In 1993, my dad had moved my grandfather Walt from New York to California as he was not fully recovering from a colon infection that caused him to have a colostomy. I would visit him all the time in the hospital—first, when he was in Antioch and then after he was moved to a long-term care facility in Oakland. My grandfather ended up passing away just a couple of nights before Dina, Megan, and I were to set off on our drive to Michigan. We were actually sleeping on the living room floor as everything else was packed up when I got the call from my dad.

The funeral was going to be in New York, and I was thinking about ways to make the funeral, maybe driving to Oklahoma and then flying to New York for the funeral and then flying back right away. Unfortunately, we had a date that we had to meet the moving van in Midland. I never could work out any arrangements and thus did not attend his funeral. I feel bad about that, but I know deep down my grandfather understood.

The day to leave for our new life in Michigan arrived. Again, as if it were yesterday, I vividly remember pulling out of our driveway in Antioch and pausing one last time in front of our house to grab one last view before we started on our new journey, the next chapter of our lives.

The drive to Michigan was magical and fun as we made the most of it and stopped at various cities and attractions we wanted to see along the way. Finally, on April 30, 1994, Dina's twenty-sixth birthday, we arrived in Midland, Michigan.

The final piece of furniture had been unloaded from the moving van, and finally Dina and I could relax. We were finally moved into the new house we were renting in Midland and all our belongings had been delivered. We wondered, what would we do now? We knew nothing about the new city we were living in. The only knowledge we gained was when we visited Midland for a house-hunting trip after I accepted my new role. Here is where Jesus once again interjected in our lives, and I am so grateful that he did. We decided to become parishioners at Blessed Sacrament Parish in Midland. We felt like this would be a great way for us to get to know people and become part of the community, and were we ever right!

The church embraced us as we embraced it. The church community was wonderful and gave us plenty of opportunities to get involved. Dina joined the mothers' group at Blessed Sacrament, which I was so happy for as she made a lot of friends in this group who really allowed her and Megan to transition into our new life in Midland. Jesus was still working for us, helping us make this next move in our journey, and I am reminded about what I wrote in my Engagement Encounter journal years earlier, "It gives Dina a little pat to going to church. Possibly that could be part of our relationship. It might bring an 'element' in our lives that we need other than each other." Amazing!

My new job at Dow was also going very well. I loved the work and the people I was working with. Many of the engineers I worked with were around the same age as I was, and they also came from all over the country to work in Midland for Dow, which allowed me to learn quite a bit from their previous experiences, which was helpful. It seemed everywhere Dina and I turned, people were so welcoming and helpful!

Since Dina had a caesarean with the birth of Megan, the doctors had scheduled a caesarean for mid-December for our second child, thinking it too would most likely have to be birthed in this manner. However, on December 3, 1994, Dina's water broke, and off to the hospital we went. After a long night at the hospital, the next day, Dina gave natural birth to our second beautiful daughter, Marisa Kaye!

Not having the privilege of seeing a natural birth with Megan, experiencing this with Marisa was amazing. To see a human being pushed out of another human being is quite honestly a miracle and one where you truly feel the presence of the Lord. That was quite a spectacular day. I never would have thought, with all the wrong that I had done in my life, I would be rewarded with such treasures. Jesus is forgiving, Jesus is loving, Jesus is *great*!

When we returned home with Marisa, I was surprised to see people from Dina's mothers' group bringing meals to our house for the first couple of weeks after Marisa was born. I was truly amazed. We had only been living in Midland a little over seven months, and our new community had embraced us and was supporting us like we had been there for years. Beautiful blessings by beautiful people.

Mental Stability

My sister Tricia had a bird that my parents had bought her that lived in its cage that hung in the corner of the kitchen. The bird's name was Tweety and for the most part was a good pet. The only time Tweety caused problems was when my parents would clean her cage and Tweety would escape from whoever was holding her during this time and start flying around the house. As kids, we loved this and laughed as we watched my parents try to corral the freed bird.

One day, when only my dad and I were home, my dad decided to clean the birdcage. Since I was the only other person home, my dad put oven mitts on my hands and had me hold the bird while he cleaned the cage. He told me, "Hold that bird tight. I don't want it flying around the house." I obeyed and tightly held Tweety while my dad cleaned the cage. When my dad finished cleaning the cage, he reached over to get Tweety from me, and he noticed that she was limp. In fact, Tweety was dead!

I didn't even notice until my dad saw the limp bird in between my oven mitts. I was just focused on being a good son and holding the bird tight so it didn't fly around the house. I was obviously bawling right then as my dad said, "You need to go bury it." He found an empty matchbox and put Tweety inside and told me to go out into the backyard and bury it.

Of course it was raining extremely hard during this time, so there I was digging a plot for Tweety in my backyard in the rain, crying profusely. I buried the bird and came back inside, still crying. I felt terrible that I killed my sister's bird.

I don't exactly remember my sister's reaction to this when she came home, although I am sure she was upset. I do remember that we left the birdcage hanging in the kitchen for a period of time afterward for some reason, and I always thought of Tweety every time I looked at that empty cage.

When I accepted the move by Dow to Midland in 1994, I knew I would have to continue going to college. That was the basis of the transfer after all. So soon after moving to Midland, I started taking college classes at a local junior college named Delta College. The first class that I enrolled in was an inorganic chemistry class. It was a little embarrassing when I found out there was a Dow plant operator in the same chemistry class with me. This operator was very inquisitive about how I could be a salary person and not have already have taken chemistry, much less not already have an associate's degree yet?

There was also a rumbling in the department I was working in at Dow as to why I was transferred. Dow typically did not transfer technologists, an employee with two-year associate's degrees. Some employees thought my wife was a Dow bigwig and I just got transferred as part of her deal. I assured them—and lied to many of them—that I was a technologist and had two years of college. So you can understand how very nervous I was that I would see my classmate at work and then perhaps the word would spread that I was taking classes at Delta and people might find out I don't have my associate's degree! Fortunately for me, however, I never did see him at work.

After completing several classes at Delta College, I then took a class at Saginaw Valley State University. It was at this point in time I really needed to decide what I wanted to major in. If I wanted to be a chemical engineer, I most likely would need to take a leave of absence from Dow Chemical and go to Michigan State to get my degree. If I wanted to get a bachelor's degree in chemistry, I could do that at Saginaw Valley State. Both of these options would take me away from what was and still is the most important part of my life, my family.

As a result of truly understanding what was important to me, I decided that I would strive for a nontechnical bachelor's degree through Northwood University in Midland. Northwood was the best school option for me as it allowed me to take classes remotely— that is, at home rather than in a classroom setting. This way, with work and a family, I could still fit school into my schedule when it was the most convenient. Furthermore, Northwood gave me "work-life credit" for my work and life experiences that I could prove, via documentation, were at or above the level of the classes I had to take. This option, I felt, would give me the best opportunity to spend the most time with my family and get my bachelor's degree in a reasonable amount of time. I truly felt that as long as I had my bachelor's degree, regardless of what I majored in, it would give me the credibility to continue to climb in the company.

As with all the college classes I had taken from the three previous colleges I attended, Dow was there to pick up the tuition for me. Dow has a philosophy that paying for one's tuition is essentially an investment in that employee, which Dow will get a long return on when that higher-educated employee gives back through their work at Dow. As far as I was concerned, it sure sounded like a win-win all around.

Work was busy but was going extremely well. My job included working independently on process research in a laboratory environment, writing batch operating procedures, overseeing specific pilot plant operations, and conducting in-process analytical for related pilot plant campaigns. In this role I authored or coauthored nine formal research reports. Furthermore, I also had the opportunity to work on a project to convert an existing Dow facility to pharmaceutical standards and then produce quality pharmaceutical product in that facility. For this project work, I was awarded the Business Performance Excellent Award in 1997.

Family life was awesome as well as we recently had purchased our first Midland home at 509 Capitol Drive. Megan was now four years old and Marisa was two, and they were the cutest little girls who loved each other so much. In addition, we found out Dina was pregnant again! I continually felt blessed with the loving family God had provided me.

Completing college coursework while also working full time, as well as having a wife and children, was extremely difficult. I had been feeling a tremendous amount of pressure to get everything done in my life that needed to be done. One Saturday morning in 1997, the burden became too heavy, and I had an emotional breakdown. I had been working on one of my class papers on my computer in the basement like I typically did on Saturday mornings. This day, however, the pressure became too much; and I walked upstairs to the kitchen and started crying and told Dina, "I just can't do this anymore."

After the breakdown, Dina convinced me that I needed to seek help from a professional therapist. She had felt for some time something was wrong. I totally balked at this idea. There was no way I was going to go into some guy's office and share my deepest, darkest feelings. Dina convinced me to at least try it, and I am so very glad I did.

I felt very comfortable with the male therapist who led me to share my life story with him over the first few sessions I had with him. I came to trust the therapist and do the very things I said I would never do. I shared my deepest, darkest feelings, and yes, I even cried in the guy's office. Following the sharing of my story, the therapist thought I had two big issues that were hindering me. The first was my parent's divorce and the effect that had on me and the second was he thought I had obsessive compulsive disorder (OCD).

The first item the therapist stated is what made me cry. I really didn't think that the divorce of my parents had a long-lasting effect on me, but the therapist pointed out several examples of how I personally held a lot of resentment of the divorce. Further sessions with the therapist helped me with this baggage that I unknowingly was carrying. With regard to the second item, OCD, I honestly was not surprised, as I had started to conclude I had OCD prior to meeting with the therapist.

Although the OCD problem never became truly serious until I was an adult, there were several things that happened when I was a child that I now think were OCD related. First off, I had many bouts of strep throat as a young child, which some doctors now believe is linked to OCD. I came to find out I also had a much labored, hard birth, which also is a speculated contributor, and I was also an extremely nervous boy. I also had these bouts where sometimes my body would strangely freeze up, and I felt like I couldn't move. I know this sounds extremely weird, but I can't find a better way to describe it. My parents would take me to the hospital every time this happened, but the doctors could never ever find anything wrong with me.

Also as a child, I kept my room very clean and would always look under my bed before going to sleep. I also started to notice during this time that I had this habit of always running numbers or words through my head repeatedly. For example, in our living room, there was a bookshelf packed full of paperback books. Whenever I sat in that room, I would have to—or so I thought—say in my head four or five book titles repeatedly, over and over again, matching the order of how they were aligned on the bookshelf. It was just something I had to do, and over time started to do even when I was not in that room.

I also had a fascination with sharp objects and the potential damage they could cause. One time, my mom just sharpened a steak knife and asked me to bring it from the counter to my dad at the kitchen table, and I decided to see how sharp the knife was by running it across my right thumb, slicing my thumb open and having to get several stitches. I also used to visualize the top edge of the freeway guard rails cutting under my eyes as I rode with my parents on the highway. I know this is hard to understand, I know this is weird, but it happened.

Of course, the things I remembered about my childhood were in hindsight of finding out I had OCD. Whether those things were OCD related or not, I cannot say for sure. I can only say it was my opinion that they were. As an adult, it wasn't until I bought my first house that I started to exhibit some OCD behaviors. Those behaviors were typically checking all the windows at night to ensure they were locked as well as checking, double-checking, and triple-checking that the doors were shut and locked and the gas knobs on the oven were in the Off position. I eventually started to put chairs by the door so if anyone ever broke in, I would hear them stumble. Sounds crazy, I know.

When I moved to Michigan, the situation got really bad. As we started to go back to church and it became a big part of our lives, I found myself continually blessing myself. When at church, I would find myself mentally calling Jesus names or cursing or doubting Jesus. This mental act really put a strain on me, and I wondered why that was happening. I found out that this is a symptom of OCD, amazingly enough.

I also could not read anything without counting the number of letters in the words I was reading. I still checked the oven, windows, and doors each night, as well as now also daily checking all the smoke detectors and carbon monoxide monitors in the house. Other things I would do are to constantly touch the top of the pictures of my kids in my office at work. I remember sitting in my office at work during this time, looking out the window, asking myself what the hell was going on with me.

Perhaps the most straining feature of OCD was the terrible mental thoughts about my children. These thoughts were usually triggered by the media events of the day. One of the worst was during the O. J. Simpson trial and the terrible thoughts this story gave me in regard to visualizing this happening to my child. Over and over and over again in my mind. I absolutely hated it!

The visit to the therapist led to my personal physician prescribing the drug Luvox to me, which I still take today. This drug has been a miracle pill for me, virtually eliminating all the torturous mental fatigue of this grasping disease and making the quality of my life so much better.

OCD is a truly horrible disease. It can take over your life if you let it, like I let it do to me. If it wasn't for Dina pushing me to get help, I wonder if I ever would have. Did Luvox cure OCD for me? No, I still battle OCD at a much less invasive level. I am not sure if other than my parents, Dina or my kids if anyone else even knows I have OCD. It is embarrassing, or at least it was to me, especially the terrible, evil thoughts that come with it. It truly makes one feel like they are insane.

As the OCD came under control, I was able to proceed forward with my life. On June 30, 1997, Dina gave natural birth to our son, Jordan Thomas. It was pretty scary when Jordan was born as they rushed him into an oxygen tank to help with his breathing and kept him in there for a day or so, but thank the Lord he was fine. He had jaundice as well and would need to have light therapy for a period of time, but again everything turned out great.

Work also continued to go well. In January 1998, I accepted a position as the pharmaceutical pilot plant operations specialist at Dow's pharmaceutical pilot plant in Midland. This upward job career move allowed me to move off the technologist career ladder and onto the engineer/chemist ladder. In this new role, I oversaw the day-to-day operation of the pharmaceutical pilot plant. The primary role of this job was to lead the effort in prioritizing and managing key pilot plant activities. Other responsibilities included organizing the plant operating procedures, being the primary computer programmer for the plant, overseeing and managing the capital spending process, and leading the effort to manage plant logistics. Furthermore, I was able to follow through on a personal mission to learn work processes from other manufacturing plants in our business. In 1999, I led a small group from the Midland pharmaceutical pilot plant to visit Dow's manufacturing plant in Freeport, Texas. During this trip, we collected valuable work process learnings that we were able to implement into the pharmaceutical pilot plant in Midland.

In January 2000, I accepted a position as a project manager for a capital improvement project at Dow's pharmaceutical manufacturing facility in Midland. The core team consisted of 13 total members, most of which were plant operators and plant and site engineers. This project was created to dramatically improve the pharmaceutical manufacturing facility's environmental performance that had not been able to achieve Dow's expected performance. The project team spent over 1.2 million dollars in capital improvements as well as improved plant procedures, plant training, and plant safety issues to complete this effort. The business recognized the team by allowing the team to share their success story at the business Quarterly Global Communications Meeting.

In August 2000, I was accepted into the Dow Chemical Six Sigma Program as a Black Belt. At the time, there were only about 1,000 Black Belts in the Dow Chemical Company globally. In the role of the Black Belt, over a total period of two years, I would need to use the Six Sigma breakthrough methodology to save at least $250,000 per project that I work on for Dow Chemical. To train a person on the Six Sigma Methodology, Dow Chemical sent all the new Black Belts from around the world to Atlanta, Georgia, for four full weeks of training.

With regard to school, the flexibility Northwood gave me was awesome. As I got closer to completing my schoolwork, I did start taking two to three classes at a time to expedite my completion. To complete the program, I needed to do an exit interview with two professors at the school. The review went extremely well, and I will never forget what one of the professors told me at the end of the review. He told me, "I am sure we haven't heard the last from you." Words I have never forgotten.

New Beginnings

It's really amazing to me how vividly I can remember my childhood days prior to my parents' divorce. It really was a special time in my life. No real responsibilities, other than school, and the focus was on building relationships with other kids and having fun. We used our imagination often, whether it was me and my friends playing the Yankees in baseball or making up a new game or activity to not be bored. We got to know the adults who lived on our street, and in turn they got to know us too. It not only was our playground but perhaps more like our extended family as well. I still keep in contact today, via social media, with many of my friends and even the adults who lived in our neighborhood. Those were memorable times living at 4300 Hilltop Drive.

In 2000, I learned my grandmother Kay was sick with cancer. I decided to travel back and see her one more time, and I brought Jordan with me so he could have a memory of his great-grandmother. Going back to visit my grandmother Kay for the last time was very hard. We had a good visit as we talked about genealogy, history, and shared stories. One of those stories she shared with me was in regard to the terrible pain she suffered when she lost her child and how her and my grandpa had tough marital times after the loss of Julie Ann, but they stuck together.

One of the tougher moments was having to say goodbye for the final time, knowing that she was soon to pass, and this was the last time we were going to visit. One thing I will never forget and can still visualize today is me pulling out of her back driveway and looking up at her bedroom window, like I always did when I left her house, to see her again looking out of the window, waving at me—that time, both of us knew it would be for the last time. Tears filled my eyes as I drove down Hilltop Drive past 4300 Hilltop Drive and toward Interstate 80 when this song came on. I don't even remember the name of the song, but I had never heard it before but it talked about memories as if she had sent that song to me. My grandma Kay was a great person. All in all, I have so much admiration for my grandparents. I am so lucky to have been a part of their lives. They were just awesome people.

My grandmother Kay died on March 27, 2001. There was never a doubt that I was going to eulogize her. I knew how much she loved what I said about my grandpa Tom, and I certainly wanted to honor her as well. This is what I shared at her rosary on April 2, 2001:

> As many of you know, people like my Grandmother only come along every so often. To me, my Grandmother was much more than just a Grandmother—she was my friend, a really close friend. From the day I was born, I lived only a mile or so from my Grandparents' house, and thus they were always a part of my life. That continued throughout my life to even the last seven years that I've lived in Michigan, we talked weekly. I cherished my relationship with her and felt it was a privilege for me to get to know her the way I did.
>
> My Grandmother was an amazingly strong person as she had many struggles over the course of her life to overcome. I want to share just a few of these with you.
>
> Her first struggle was when, as a young child living in Ireland, she went with her Aunt on an extended trip to the United States. As my

Grandmother battled with a severe case of childhood asthma, doctors thought the air quality and the doctors in the United States would help her. Unfortunately for my Grandmother, for various reasons, the extended stay became a permanent stay, and she was never able to return home to her family.

After my Grandmother married my Grandfather Tom, their first child Julie Ann passed away at less than two years of age from cystic fibrosis disease. Just in recent months, my Grandmother shared with me the awful pain she felt in losing this child and how tough it was on her marriage. But love and faith prevailed, and she and my Grandfather was thankfully able to have three more healthy children.

My Grandfather Tom battled many various ailments up to the time he passed away about eight years ago. My Grandmother was the best nurse that our family has ever seen. For years, not only did she continue working at her normal Catholic diocesan job as a bookkeeper, but she spent her off-hours tending to my Grandfather. It was truly an amazing and very inspirational thing to see. What would we have done without her?

Though faced with these many struggles in her life, my Grandmother used her strong faith and love to overcome them and in fact focused much more on the many, many positive and fun moments she had. I now want to just share a couple of those fun moments that I experienced with her.

About ten years or so ago, the family had gathered at my Grandparents' house for Thanksgiving dinner. While preparing the turkey, my Grandmother accidentally sliced her hand, bad enough to where she most likely needed stitches. Grandma did not want to ruin dinner and instead heavily wrapped up the thumb to slow the bleeding during dinner. She also forbid anyone to tell Grandpa during this time as he would surely get upset and make her go to the hospital. So there we all sat eating dinner, Grandma one handed and everyone being more quiet than usual until out the blue, Bob says, "Everyone who likes the turkey, raise your hand!" Bob followed with several other questions prompting everyone to raise their hand. Everyone at the table laughed so hard except for Grandpa who couldn't figure out what the heck was going on and was probably wondering if his entire family had gone goofy.

Another time, after probably not getting my way as a twelve-year-old, I ran away from home one day. I left my house and walked about a mile to my Grandmother's house. I went and hid behind my Grandpa's old Chevy that was permanently parked on the side of the house. Unbeknown to me, my Mom had called my Dad home from work and even contacted my Grandmother about my running away. I hid there behind the Chevy for what seemed as an eternity. One moment I decided to stand up, and as soon as I did, my Grandma came driving her green Dodge Dart down the driveway and saw me right away. I can still picture the eye contact we made at each other until this day. I was busted! For some reason, this became a memorable event in both my Grandmother's and my eyes as just recently we laughed together about our memories of this event.

I am going to miss my Grandmother. I am going to miss talking to her on the phone. In a short five- or ten-minute discussion with

Grandma, I could get updates on how all the family members were doing—even some I never had met before. Speaking of which, I am going to also miss hearing Grandma talk about Ireland, her recent visits and/or upcoming trips to Ireland. She so loved Ireland. I am going to miss visiting my Grandparents' house. It was such a truly welcoming home, and I have so many memories from that place. But most of all, I am going to miss a very good friend of mine—and that hurts.

Grandma was always there for you if you needed help. She was also very proud of her family and would love to brag, and brag, and brag about her family members! I also found my Grandmother to be a great source to funnel prayer requests through. I figured with her spiritual life, her lengthy commitment to working for the church, and all the connections she had with the many priests and sisters she had made friends with over the years, she had to have some heavy hay points with God. I figured it was as close to a direct line to God as one could get. And you know what, when she prayed for something, the results were astounding!

You know, when my Grandmother visited Ireland, I don't think she ever sat in first class, but I feel confident that she sat in the first row of first class when she took the nonstop charter flight to heaven last week. If she didn't, I don't know of anyone else who would have a chance!

Thanks, Grandma! I love you!

My grandmother Kay was my last living grandparent and was truly a mentor and a friend, in addition to being my grandmother. I know she is looking down upon her family, blessing and protecting us as well as praying for us nonstop.

In 2002, Dina and I bought the home we would raise our children in. We moved to 508 Wanetah Drive in Midland, and I hoped this would be the house and the neighborhood that my kids would one day remember so fondly, like I did of 4300 Hilltop Drive.

Later that year, after about eight years of college courses, I finally graduated cum laude from Northwood University with a bachelor's degree in business management in May 2002. I wasn't keen on going through the graduation ceremony, but Dina really wanted me to. I realized that this accomplishment was something we achieved together. Dina sacrificed a lot in her life for me to finish school as well, and she was right—it was a huge milestone. I did walk in the graduation ceremony, and I am very glad I did.

With a degree in tow, I will spend the next seventeen years being the best father and husband I can be. I made my family the priority over everything else in life. I tried to attend every practice, game, or event for dance, cheer, lacrosse, softball, baseball, football, basketball, soccer, tennis, swim, gymnastics, golf, track, cross country, ice hockey, figure skating, roller skating, academics, and drama that I could. I am proud of my attendance record as there wasn't much that I missed.

In addition, I got to spend time with my kids and coach them for years in various sports. This was a win-win for me. Spending time with them is always great, but I love to coach and I really enjoyed those opportunities to have a positive impact on other young kids as well.

I am proud to say that all my children graduated college. Megan attended the Culinary Institute of America in Hyde Park, New York, and received her bachelor's degree in culinary arts. She is married to Adrian, who she met at college, and they have a beautiful baby daughter named Ava. Megan works for MGM Grand as an assistant manager in one of their restaurants in Las Vegas, Nevada. Marisa attended Ferris State University in Big Rapids, Michigan, and received her bachelor's degree in early childhood education. She currently is engaged to her fiancé Dan and works as a teacher in Grand Rapids, Michigan. Jordan attended Delta Community College for one year to play baseball but transferred to the University of Michigan in his sophomore year and received his bachelor's degree in political science.

Jordan has a girlfriend, Andrea, and works for CBRE Commercial Real Estate Services in Chicago, Illinois.

Dina and I are empty nesters still living at 508 Wanetah Drive. Dina works for Edward Jones Financial in Midland, and I still work for Dow. I did reach my desired role of people leader and have been one now for twelve years and absolutely love it. Our conversations these days are mostly around planning for retirement, which we hope to do in another two to three years. Oh, and by the way, as mentioned several times, I love this lady more today than ever. She is truly an amazing person, and I am so thankful our paths in life lined up.

I have a good relationship with my parents and my siblings. My mom and Gary are still married and live in Arizona, while my dad and Cheri are still married and live in Michigan. I talk to both my mom and dad about once a week, and Dina and I try to have dinner with my dad and Cheri every couple of months since they live only a couple of hours away from Midland.

I know the perception I give in this book was not always flattering to my stepparents Gary or Cheri. Please know that was my perception at the time, a period where my mom and dad were going their own ways, and I did not like it. Regardless of who it was that started to date or marry either of my parents, I am sure I would have acted the same way. I love both Gary and Cheri, and they have been supportive, loving people who love my mom and dad respectively. And for that, I am grateful. I truly apologize to both of them for my behavior toward them earlier in my life.

For the rest of my immediate family, Tricia has one son and a granddaughter as well as a longtime boyfriend and lives in Oregon. John is married and has three boys and lives in Arizona. Jim is married and has two daughters and a son and lives in Arizona. Angela is married and has a son and a daughter and lives in Arizona.

If you sense a theme of everyone living outside of California now, you would be correct. Even Dina's parents, Gary and Estelle, now live in Nevada as well. Although I have been out of California now for more than twenty-five years, I will always have a piece of it with me. Especially those years at 4300 Hilltop Drive, where innocence ruled and happy memories were made.

No Regrets

There are a few things I want people to take away from this book. First and foremost, I am not a victim. One could argue and say you were molested and even shot at and had a plane crash above you—of course, you are a victim. I don't allow myself to fall into this category as I feel this is the easy way out. I feel as though those things happened and I need to learn from them and move on.

Second, I recognize there were angels put in front of me throughout my life along the path. Times that, if they weren't there, something wouldn't have happened. For example, Dina's parents allowing me to live with them after I got kicked out of the house or my supervisor at Dow who counseled me on the benefits of moving to Midland or my coworker Mark whom I met during my interview in Midland. We have been best friends now for more than twenty-five years. Trust me when I tell you there are angels out there for you as well. There have been in your past, there are now, and there will be in your future. Look around. I promise you they are there. While Jesus has a life path set out for you, I firmly belief these angels in our lives have the ability to get us back on the path when we unknowingly go astray.

Finally, we all have choices in life and can react to situations in certain ways. For me, I have had many regrets, but I use those learnings in the conversations I have with my kids and with other kids whom I coach. One big regret was quitting that high school football team. I think about that often. I can't believe I quit because I was embarrassed a coach chewed me out. That decision had a lingering effect on my playing any sports moving forward. I have learned it is okay to fail, but like the kid on the bike that didn't have brakes and crashed, you need to pick yourself up and move forward.

Above all this, I firmly believe Jesus Christ is helping every one of us souls get through life's journey to accomplish the various learnings that he had set out for us to gain since birth. Maybe this is my way of justifying things, but I ask myself, *Why I didn't get caught stealing or doing drugs? Why did other people I know go to jail or prison for similar acts?* I choose to believe that jail or prison was part of their life journey. Does that mean I was better in any way than those people who got caught? Hell no! I was probably worse than some who did go to jail or prison. It is simply my belief as to why I believe I didn't get caught.

Today, I have a relationship with Jesus, and I pray to him every morning on the way to work. When I pray to Jesus, I try not to ask for things that are what I consider gifts, like help my team win this game or anything like that. I simply ask him to keep my family and I safe. Even after I pray, I leave the radio off and have quiet time on my way in to work so I can also listen to Jesus. Just from listening to Jesus, I felt the need to write this book; and now after opening my heart for this book, I still feel there is something greater Jesus wants me to do with my life. I am curious to see where Jesus leads me. I must continue to listen.

To be honest, today, our church participation is nothing like it was when we first moved to Midland. I don't feel guilty for missing church because I have this relationship with Jesus. In fact, I was getting burned out by the Catholic Church and looking for something more motivational. I found Joel Osteen to be that motivational inspiration that I was looking for, and he has enhanced my relationship with Jesus through his daily prayers and coaching that he provides via social media. I believe everyone needs to have their own unique relationship with Jesus, something that feels right for them. Church is certainly an option; it is a celebration of community with Jesus. However, I think there are other mechanisms for having a relationship with Jesus as well, and I pray that everyone reading this today finds their way and accepts Jesus as their Savior and develops a personal relationship with him.

Since we just mentioned it above, let's talk about drugs. My drug of choice was methamphetamine. During my teenage years, where I lived, methamphetamine seemed to be the popular drug of choice, much like marijuana in the '60s and like heroin in the present day. I have become a believer that illegal drugs are created by the devil—through man, obviously, but by the devil. Think about all the wrong in this world and how drugs play a part in it. Whether someone kills someone or steals from someone or even abuses someone, drugs often play a role. Imagine for minute if illegal drugs were not in this world. Think it would be a better place?

Let's chat about OCD. For all of you out there who suffer from OCD or any other mental disability, I beg you to seek help. I admit this is a hypocritical statement by me as earlier I told you I wouldn't have sought help if Dina didn't push me that way. It's also hypocritical as even today I don't fully admit to people, even new personal doctors, that I have OCD. I never bring it up to friends, and to new doctors, I tell them I take Luvox for anxiety. Somehow that makes me feel saner. But if you or someone you know is suffering from this tremendous mental burden, I beg you to step up and be a bigger person than I was and get help. Therapists and doctors won't react to some of your thoughts like you think they will react. They have heard it before. There is help out there that can change your life for the better.

In the past, I had thought a lot about coming out and sharing my OCD story or joining a support group, but I kept this, like many other things in my life, close to the vest. I did find reading books about OCD to be very helpful, primarily because it is nice to know you are not alone.

As a child of divorce, it really does suck. It was worse experiencing it than what I thought it would be after hearing from my friends whose parents got a divorce. I don't wish any child to be a child of divorce, and when I coach young people in sports, I try to have a conversation with those kids who I know are a child of divorce. It's hard, though, because even though I can share my story, they don't see the entire picture yet. I didn't realize how much baggage I was still carrying for years after my parents' divorce until I talked to a professional. My advice here is for parents to invest in their child, if you are getting a divorce, by getting them in to talk to a professional. Believe me, you don't want them carrying that weight all those years.

I also want to talk about sexual abuse. I really don't know how bad that incident screwed me up in life or not. Did it contribute to me diving into drugs in any way or magnify the intensity of my OCD at all? I have no idea because 'til this day, the only person I have ever told is Dina and the kids. Should I have said something to someone? Yes. Would that have prevented someone from being sexually assaulted by this person in the future? Perhaps. I do live with guilt that people were assaulted after me because I didn't speak up. I didn't speak up. That's on me.

With regard to education, my life's journey has shown me the true value of what a college diploma can bring to one's life. After I finally graduated college, I vowed that I would ensure my children graduated college, and I was going to pay for it. I made this very clear from early on in life so my children knew what the expectation was. This would be a key lesson I learned from my life that I felt I could pass down and provide for my children.

I don't want anyone to think that traditional university is all that I support. I have become a firm believer in what trade schools can provide to people as well. My point here is that I support education beyond high school and hope that kids can find something they are passionate and proud about, learn it, and then have a successful career doing it. That is winning in my book! Not that I feel ashamed in anyway about my degree, but as mentioned, I had hidden my lack of education before my degree; and as I have moved up through the ranks of Dow, I still feel inferior to some of the people I work with, whom I even lead, who went to larger schools and have engineering degrees. I don't share much about myself, so I even wonder how many people I work with know my educational background. I wish it weren't this way.

I wrote this book to hopefully connect to people who are going through or have gone through some of the things I have went through in life with the hope that knowing someone else has gone through what they are dealing with; it might help them seek the help they need to get through these life issues. I also hope that people know that while it seems like things are really bad now, I sincerely hope that they accept my rationale for the path of life and that they use that as motivation to get through the tough times. I was lost, several times, before Jesus put me back down on the beach and the number of footsteps went back to four from two. Jesus will be there for you too. All you have to do is ask him to help. When it gets tough, I beg you, do not give up.

I want to end the book by saying *thank you* to the five most influential people who I feel has saved my life and save it still every day. The first is Jesus. Without my faith in the Lord and my relationship with him, there is absolutely no telling where I would be today. Second, my amazing and beautiful wife, Dina. Dina has always been there for me as my coach, my partner, my lover, and my best friend. I am so blessed to call this lady my wife! Finally, Megan, Marisa, and Jordan—thank you for loving me and letting me be a huge part of your lives. I love you all more than you will ever know and pray that you continue to grow closer to Jesus and that you continue to live your life in the positive, loving way you have since you were born. I love you!

FOOTPRINTS IN THE SAND

One night I dreamed I was walking along the beach with the Lord.
Many scenes from my life flashed across the sky.
In each scene I noticed footprints in the sand.
Sometimes there were two sets of footprints,
other times there were one set of footprints.

This bothered me because I noticed
that during the low periods of my life,
when I was suffering from
anguish, sorrow or defeat,
I could see only one set of footprints.

So I said to the Lord,
"You promised me Lord,
that if I followed you,
you would walk with me always.
But I have noticed that during
the most trying periods of my life
there have only been one
set of footprints in the sand.
Why, when I needed you most,
you have not been there for me?"

The Lord replied,
"The times when you have
seen only one set of footprints,
is when I carried you."

Mary Stevenson

ABOUT THE AUTHOR

*H*illtop Drive is the first book authored by Joe Jachens. Joe and his wife, Dina, currently live in Michigan and have three adult children. Joe can be contacted at mijoeca@yahoo.com.